#SPONSORED

# #SPONSORED

### HOW ATHLETES AND BRANDS CAN LEVERAGE EACH OTHER TO CREATE VALUE

## JASMINE CHOU

NEW DEGREE PRESS
COPYRIGHT © 2020 JASMINE CHOU
All rights reserved.

#SPONSORED
*How Athletes and Brands Can Leverage Each Other to Create Value*

| ISBN | | |
|---|---|---|
| | 978-1-64137-508-5 | *Paperback* |
| | 978-1-64137-509-2 | *Kindle Ebook* |
| | 978-1-64137-510-8 | *Ebook* |

# CONTENTS

SPECIAL KUDOS TO . . . . . . . . . . . . . . . . . . . . . 7

**CHAPTER 1.** . . . . . . . . . . . . . . . . . . . . . . . . . . . . . . . . 11
**CHAPTER 2.** GO GET 'EM, TIGER. . . . . . . . . . . . . . . . . . . 15
**CHAPTER 3.** THE BUSINESS MIND . . . . . . . . . . . . . . . . . . 29
**CHAPTER 4.** A-TEAM ASSEMBLE. . . . . . . . . . . . . . . . . . . 41
**CHAPTER 5.** IT'S A SMALL, SMALL WORLD . . . . . . . . . . . 51
**CHAPTER 6.** BRAND AMBASSADORS AS AMPLIFIERS . . . . 65
**CHAPTER 7.** SPONSOR-ATHLETE FIT . . . . . . . . . . . . . . . . 81
**CHAPTER 8.** REASSESSING THE RELATIONSHIP . . . . . . . . 97
**CHAPTER 9.** CONTENT IS KING. . . . . . . . . . . . . . . . . . . . 109
**CHAPTER 10.** FUTURE IS FEMALE. . . . . . . . . . . . . . . . . . . 129
**CHAPTER 11.** . . . . . . . . . . . . . . . . . . . . . . . . . . . . . . . . 141

APPENDIX . . . . . . . . . . . . . . . . . . . . . . . . . . 145

# SPECIAL KUDOS TO

Albert Shih, PhD
Alexander Wong
Allison Reed
Amie Chen
Angela Chang
Angela Chu
Ann Wang
Annie Chang
Annie Xie
Arnold Tao
Brad Hunter
Chen-Yi Wu
Cherry Tseng
Christian Pluchino
Cody Hsu
Cory Rose
Daniel Sun
David Solodukho
Dennis Liao
Derek Lou
Diane Wang

Dustin Soliven
Elisa Ting
Elizabeth Mahoney
Ellen Jen
Emily Pang
Emmanuel Kontokalos
Enting Chu
Eric Koester
Erica Liu, MD
Erika Sporkert
Erin Ladendorf
Eva Yiin
Frank Fan
Fu-Nien Wang, PhD
Hao Huang
Hong Xu
Isabel Tseng
Isabel Yang
Isabelle Dickens
Ivy Shen
Jamie Shih

Jason Shih
Jeannine Mahoney
Jeff Chen
Jeffrey Bale
Jennie Wang
Jennifer Comfort
Jeremy Kitchen
Jerry Bartolome
Jerry Wang
Jesse Shih
Jessica Chou
Jessica McCarter
Joan Stepler
Joanna Chang
Joanne Yang
Joe Dorff
Joseph Wei
Joyce Huang
Julie Shih
Juo-Wei Wu
Justin Mortensen
Kate Kistler Patterson
Li Guo
Liang Koh
Liv Devitt
Louie Bacaj
Lyndze Blosser
Matthew De Silva
Michael Brimer
Michael Chen
Mischa Irsch
Morgan Williams

Peter Wang
Renee Huang
Richard McDermott
Robert Walker
Sally Wang
Sam Hsu
Sean Campbell
Simon Tang
Skanda Mohan
Sophia Tseng
Stephanie Flores
Tiffany Chou
Titan Kuo
Tony Huang
Tzu-Yun Wang
Vicky Gu
Walter Lin
Wendy Lin
Wong Ka Francis Wai
Yang-Chih Tan
Yazata Bhote
Yu-Shin Tan
Yumi Chiang
丁嘉昱
王有銘
王婕
王筠
王語
王小花
王威博士
毛琪瑛醫師
李紹唐講師

| | |
|---|---|
| 汪士林 | 孫鐵軍 |
| 李淑如 | 黃明朝 |
| 周廷駿 | 黃美雲 |
| 周耀訪 | 許小野 |
| 周秀華 | 許富華講師 |
| 周秀美 | 張紹康 |
| 周慧君 | 陳宗仁醫師 |
| 周慧玲 | 程美文 |
| 林家祥 | 詹偉文 |
| 林祐華 | 鄭梅合 |
| 林育辛 | 楊川川 |
| 林巧淇 | 楊茂勳醫師 |
| 林貴珠 | 楊雅文 |
| 林蓮華 | 蔡娟娟 |
| 范並煌 | 蔣永昌 |
| 范文綱 | 蔣筱薇 |
| 范誠宗醫師 | 歐水月 |
| 洪松葉 | 圓桌教育基金會 |

# ONE

Imagine footsteps pounding pavement in the concrete jungle. A flutter of bodies zipping through the urban backdrop. The streets are fully alive and breathing, cars are honking along, and packs of runners are racing through the city streets from point A to B. This is an unsanctioned race. No road closures exist, and safety is self-determined. This is the antithesis of large manicured running events. If you look closely, there may be a flash of a logo, maybe subtle or overt from the apparel, or from the matching shoes on the racers' feet.

The running crew revolution, a counter to traditional running, started a decade prior in 2004, which was the founding of one of the oldest New York City manifestation of run crews, BridgeRunners. The original NYC run crew began as nightly workouts attracting people from all walks of life. The name BridgeRunners came from routes consisting of running across one of the many bridges in downtown Manhattan.[1]

Coming out of the unstructured nighttime runs bridging culture and running, Knox Robinson and Jessie Zapo took an idea and ran with it. In 2013, Knox and Jessie kicked off a workout with a few friends and a couple of followers from

---

1   Meg Lappe, "Inside the Black Roses: NYC's Fastest and Most Elusive Run Club," Gear Patrol (Gear Patrol, May 10, 2018).

BridgeRunners, and Black Roses was born. Both groups were part of a generation of run crews that made their mark against the grain of traditional running clubs.

Clubs were traditionally centered around structured workouts focused on individual athletic aspirations, whereas crews focused on the collective and the culture, but not necessarily forgoing speed by any means. The historically homogenous, Caucasian, and male-majority clubs saw the unassuming disruption of a diverse band of rebels injecting street culture into running. The allure of running through urban settings, partaking in unsanctioned races, or just the rawness of running was enough commonality to congregate a band of misfits in cities all over the world. "It's more about running as an expression, like any art form," Knox Robinson, the founder of Black Roses, described in a later interview.[2]

The melding of the streets and the sport, iconic to run crews, attracted Nike, Under Armour, and Adidas to participate in this culture. These brands have sponsored crews and/or incorporated them into ad assets.[3] The Nike Swoosh is commonplace on most Black Roses gear. Over the years, other brands have accompanied the crew. In 2018, Jaybird, a headphone company, featured Knox in a series of short films titled *Run Wild*.[4] Black Roses had a whole featured film in the series. It's hard not to notice the hints of the best brands such as Maurten, a top of the line sport nutrition brand;

---

2   Adam Elder, "The Rise of Run Crews," Motiv Sports, (Motiv Sports, December 4, 2017).

3   Ibid.

4   "Chapter 5: Grit," Run Wild (Jay Bird, November 2018).

District Vision, performance eyewear; and Nike, as part of the team's accessories.

Flash forward to present day, and there is still a distinct look and feel for these crews. I was curious as to how a small band of counter-culturists could have highly credible partnerships. For Black Roses, these are the best products for arguably one of the best run crews. The brand, aesthetic, collective image, and whatever nomenclature that became part of the lexicon is intentional. The crew's brand centricity isn't unique to only Black Roses either. In the film series *Run Wild*, run crews from London, New York, and Japan embody running culture aesthetic. It's part of their run crew brand and identity.

These brand sponsors are happy to sponsor run crews that present their identity in this way. These run crews aren't pros, signaling shifts in athletic sponsorship over the years. In the modern paradigm, nonprofessional athletes attaining sponsorship isn't a stretch of the imagination. Social media has changed the fabric of life, essentially democratizing who can have influence. This allows athletes to hone into their value proposition. On the other side, the digital revolution has also given brands more efficient marketing tactics to reach a wider audience, target specific customer groups, and drastically increase the return on marketing investment.

Initially, I had doubts that as a mid-tier athlete I could get sponsored. In 2018, I had just picked up a new sport and was beginning to understand the high cost associated with competing at the level that I aspired to. This book is the product of the work I did to understand how to leverage the current state of sports sponsorship. The next chapters are the culmination of a multiyear endeavor to process my learnings and interest in amateur sports sponsorship. I believe these stories will help elite athletes and nonathletes alike understand how brands and athletes can leverage each other and, what the sponsor-sponsored relationship means.

Sponsorship today is driven by collaboration providing benefits for both sides. To take advantage of this, athletes need to understand how the process works and how they can benefit from it. In the first couple chapters, amateur athletes can use certain mindsets to help them help themselves. In the next section, I pull back the curtain to understand how brands can increase their rate of success when they invest in athletes. Understanding the rationale behind why brands sponsor can also help prospective athletes. Lastly, I delve into the future of sport sponsorship and the increasing shift toward female sponsorship and equality in sports. Ultimately, elite amateurs and brands can both significantly benefit from investing in the sponsorship relationship.

## TWO

# GO GET 'EM, TIGER

---

"Go get 'em, tiger" has always been a call to action for me. It's that little nudge to get started on something. Before thinking about attaining sponsorships, it's imperative to toe the start line, race, and build the record.

### ZERO TO SIXTY

You should know something about me. When I'm mentally committed to something, I'm 110 percent in. My triathlon career has been short and sweet, trending toward smarter and more consistent. Really, I went zero to sixty at lightning speed. I will be the first to admit, I only put enough thought into hitting the purchase button to race entries but never overthought or second-guessed my decisions. Looking back on my seasons, any triathlon veteran would question why I jumped into the full Ironman distance within my first triathlon season and how I justified doing four 140.6-mile races within twelve months directly after. Youth and rookie naïveté, along with conviction and just the right amount of crazy, has gotten me this far and to the most renowned Ironman distance race, Kona.

In the fall of 2017, I won my age group (age classification in triathlon) at the Mighty Man Montauk Olympic. The only reason I had signed up for Montauk was because my best friend wanted to do a half-Ironman (70.3 miles) that summer and I couldn't accommodate her schedule. Instead, I decided to do a small race at the end of the triathlon season in the fall. I did well enough that the next year I embarked on my first season, finishing four Olympic-distance races, one half, and one full Ironman.

Halfway through my first season, I talked myself into signing up for Ironman Taiwan in the summer of 2018. It was in a charming Victorian house that I mentally committed to chase that elusive Kona or Ironman World Championship slot. To do so meant that I would have to win my age group at one of the Ironman races hosted around the world. I reckoned I had the best chance of qualifying in the 18–24 age group, as competition gets exponentially stiffer in the 25–29 and 30–34 age groups. There, at a high school basketball team reunion in San Diego, California, I also convinced my best friend to try and qualify for Kona with me.

Fast forward three months later, I was headed to Taiwan for my first Ironman race. More specifically, I was headed to a tiny rural island of the Penghu archipelago, off the western coast of Taiwan. A local friend was nice enough to let me borrow her time trial (TT) bike, a bike made for increased triathlon aerodynamics. She was flabbergasted I was racing on a bike I had never ridden before, much less a time trial bike where the aggressive positioning would make six plus hours on the bike saddle miserable. Again, I had no idea what I was signing myself up for. I was lucky enough to have the support of my extended family and a few friends. We bunked in a three-story Airbnb as our home base as I swam, biked, and ran around the tiny, super windy island.

Come race day, the brilliant neon bridge stretching over swim start did not subdue my Ironman debut nerves. Not surprisingly, I was a complete mess; I didn't respond to any of my fifteen family members and blocked out all stimuli. There were hordes and hordes of people milling around the small pathway into the harbor. The October temperature was slightly too hot to be comfortable in a neoprene triathlon wetsuit specifically made for the water. To add to the morning havoc, high winds gave ample reason for the race organizers to shorten the 3,800-meter swim to 400 meters. Race start was then pushed back another hour, even as all the athletes were already getting antsy. Sooner or later I eventually slotted myself in the back of the waves of people heading to swim start. The start of the race was self-selected for each athlete, and my race time would start when I crossed the first timing sensor. As I stood in the sardine-packed corrals, I zeroed in on the one competitor I knew was vying for the same Kona slot. One by one, athletes went down the spiky staircases into the water.

When I got through the human funnel and after I treaded lightly down the staircase, I was met by older athletes doing doggy-style and breaststrokes to start off their swim. After a few minutes of wave tumbling and swimming into rope lines, I hobbled back up the staircase. Out of the choppy waters, the bike leg was absolutely brutal. Not only were the roads not closed, meaning traffic was flowing as usual, but I also had to deal with the unforgiving elements. With every turn, while trying to make sense of the poor road markers, I had heightened awareness of being hit by a car/moped or being undercut by bursts of wind. I also didn't set up my hydration properly, forcing me to stop at every aid station. Halfway through the race, my left fourth toe was aching so badly I really thought I broke a bone. The only bright side with the open roads and the poorly secured bike route was that my friends, who followed me on two mopeds, provided a little moral support. By the run, I was blessed to hit stride with another athlete. She got me through the marathon, and I ended up finishing in second place in my age group.

I returned back to the states to sign up for three Ironman races in 2019. Again, I had no experience to caution against what a terrible idea that was. Up until now, I was mostly training in 80 square feet of personal space. But I was smart enough to realize I needed major help by the new year. The Wattie Ink Elite Team, a sponsored triathlon team backed by a multisport clothing brand, saw something in me and offered me a spot on the team. I joined Purple Patch Fitness, a coaching organization and community under Matt Dixon and started working with a coach.

Next stop was Ironman New Zealand in March 2019, in the lake town of Taupo. After a brief introduction to my coach, my timeline forced us to jump right into the build phase, or the training period, where I put in the most work to get stronger and faster. I had just a little over two months to buy my own TT bike, figure out a racing strategy, and learn how to work with a new coach.

A couple weeks out, Bike Flights/FedEx destroyed the TT bike I bought from Colorado in shipping. I got a last-minute bike fit and adjustment done on a road bike, a more all-around bike not specifically equipped for triathlon racing. To make do, I added clip-on handlebars to get me closer to the TT aerodynamic position. Not exactly the additional stress needed days before I flew halfway around the world to bunk in what resembled a glorified garage.

Ironman New Zealand was unlike anything I'd ever experienced before. Taupo welcomed the race with open arms, the complete opposite of Taiwan in support and experience. Once I somehow survived the mass swim start where all two thousand athletes went off at the sound of a cannon, the water was clear and calm, and I knew I had to chip away at the competitors on the bike and run. The rolling hills and headwinds coming back into town were all I remembered from the bike portion. The benefit of riding my road bike was that I gained comfort and confidence even if I lost aerodynamics. The triple loop run was made up of a lot of undulating hills, too. It was a highly exposed route, but the cheering was unparalleled to races I'd done before. Locals came out in droves. By the time I got onto the run, I figured I was in fourth or fifth place. I trudged along, having moments where I hit stride, but also lapses where I hit mental and physical walls. I was ecstatic by the time I was running down the finishing gauntlet. Taupo really did roll out the red carpet.

Still under the impression I finished mid-pack, my mom mentioned she saw a couple younger-looking Japanese girls finish before me. When I checked my phone for messages, I was super confused. All my friends tracking me virtually texted me congrats and started talking about Hawaii. By now it was dark, and my mom and I were standing in the middle of a field where a generator light casted a shadow. Still confused, I asked her to pull up the tracker on her phone. When she did, "1st of" came up. I was in disbelief! Mom and I started screaming and hugging as I half-exclaimed "I'm going to Kona!"

Emotions didn't settle until the next day when I got to the Roll Down Ceremony, which was where I had to confirm my acceptance of the World Champion slot. I swore there was a blip in the results.

I qualified for Kona in March of 2019. I then went on to finish Ironman Cairns in June and Ironman Santa Cruz 70.3 in September. It was a long, long season, but I was beyond excited for the last dance and victory lap of 2019. My triathlon journey had started with one race that propelled me into these crazy experiences.

**JUST RACE**

I really didn't think much about my progression. I didn't stymie myself by overthinking. I felt that if I thought too hard about the feat, I would psyche myself out of racing.

Don't think, just do. Maybe easier said than done. We've all heard the phrase "paralysis by analysis" or the inescapable Nike slogan "Just Do It."[5] The first step to amateur sports

---

5   Barbara Gail Montero, "The Myth of 'Just Do It'," The New York Times (The New York Times, June 10, 2013).

sponsorship is getting out there and racing. It's so easy to procrastinate and get caught up in self-doubt. We get stuck fixating on failing, losing, or making a fool of ourselves. Yet, that is a self-fulfilling prophecy. The more we fixate on doubt, the more we reinforce that thought. Those negative thoughts can form into belief. Brain magnetic resonance imaging has shown how our brains filter thoughts and create medical, electrochemical, and biophysical reactions to inhibit ourselves.[6] Doubt puts limits to our own potential.

Doubt and worry can go hand in hand. Having a natural propensity for loss aversion or situations with increased worry can take over the working memory (portion of brain activity engaged at once). This increases the likelihood of choking, according to research by Dr. Sian Beilock, a former psychology professor at the University of Chicago who is now president of Barnard College.[7] Additional stressors include confirming assumed stereotypes (e.g. the idea that girls aren't supposed to do so-and-so sports) or high stakes events that can take over the working mind, which diminishes the capacity to perform. Athletes can worry so much in these events that they can no longer concentrate on performing well.

Athletes with larger working memory, which in base case is advantageous, as a larger portion of the brain can be engaged to perform, can be affected in a disproportionately negative

---

[6] "With Brain Science, Doubt Can Be a Distant Memory," The Washington Post (WP Company, May 24, 2016).

[7] Susannah Locke, "The Science of Choking under Pressure—and How to Avoid It," Vox (Vox, August 4, 2016).

way when worry takes over. These athletes, who exhibit more natural talent, largely rely on the working memory of the brain for performance. When worry crowds out the working memory, it takes over that same part of the brain that they default to more so than an athlete with an average working memory to perform.[8]

So, does practice make perfect? Well, practicing with a goal might. According to Paul Baar, a psychologist at Fordham University, one of the best ways to overcome that self-doubt is to focus on a goal. Whether the goal is to complete the first race, just finish it, or just go through the learning process, use whatever vehicle necessary to get out and compete. To increase the likelihood of success, having discrete, incremental goals in the beginning, then shifting toward bigger goals at the end has a proven track record, based on research by Professor Szu-Chi Huang at Stanford Business School.[9] Maybe your first goal is just to compete in a race or go through the training process. Then, as training turns into ingrained habit, it may be more beneficial to move your sights to something bigger.

Don't overthink or get bogged down in self-doubt. Though it might seem obvious, the first step toward amateur sports sponsorship is to get out there and race, compete, or do whatever sport you love.

---

8   Ibid.

9   Barbara Gail Montero, "The Myth of 'Just Do It'," The New York Times (The New York Times, June 10, 2013).

## SALLY WANG

The incremental progress toward something bigger in the end can be seen in Sally Wang's story. The first time I met Sally Wang, she was extremely unassuming. My mom organized an extravagant Japanese omakase in Taiwan. Sally had a race in the near future, and during the dinner, we geeked out over road bikes and talked about gear. In the years that I'd known her, she didn't speak much about her past as an elite triathlon athlete. She never once mentioned dominating the podium or her unprecedented work paving the way for Taiwanese brands to see the value of individual sponsorship. At the peak of her career, she was affiliated with brands such as Nike, Giant, Lezyne, and Red Bull.

Sally came from a family of triathletes, but lacked the interest to follow in the footsteps of her parents and brother when she was younger. Her first serious consideration of the sport started in college around 2004. She joked that the desire to lose weight pushed her into training and then her routine turned into a habit. For Sally, it wasn't a meticulous strategy to become an elite athlete; the effort was a constant pursuit to get to the next level.

Sally, though, made sure to nuance the achievement of becoming an elite athlete to say it didn't make her a pro. "Elite athlete" to her meant a level, rather than an occupation, even though the training and time commitment were on par. The difference of prestige, public image, and financial security between elite competitors and professional athletes to me would be a technicality. Sally spent all her time at facilities, workshops, and international training programs in Colorado, Australia, and Africa. She trained with the likes of Olympians and world-class athletes like Gwen Jorgensen and Kiyomi Niwata.[10] From an outsider perspective, it really was a full-time job. Path dependence and a desire to be fit seemed to be a weak and insufficient reason behind a ten-year commitment to triathlons.

Her sponsorship journey started because of a loose screw. Not in her head, but on a secondhand bike. Upon being reintroduced to the sport, Sally rode her mom's vintage road bike. To maintain the seat post position, Sally jimmied the piece with tape to stop the seat post from slipping. Unfortunately, her efforts failed to keep the seat steady beneath her. She finally brought the bike into a bike shop because she thought the screw mechanism was not tightening properly. Come to find out, the seat post diameter was incorrect. At the time, she was racing more and more and felt it was appropriate to invest in a new bike. Imploring her dad for bike funds went nowhere. He wasn't convinced enough to shell out money for new equipment for his daughter's newfound interest in sports. He said she either had to work to pay for the replacement bike or get sponsored, if she had the audacity to do so.

Not used to asking for handouts, Sally wasn't comfortable asking for company freebies; however, she was inadvertently influenced by two people in her life. She had a friend who openly created fundraising campaigns to fund his own gear upgrades and travels. Coming from a modest Chinese upbringing, Sally felt there were questionable spending habits with the support her friend received. But she did note the

---

10   編輯群, "鐵人之花—汪旖文的凱旋之路," Don1Don, (Don1Don, May 7, 2018).

personal brand and marketing work. Then, there was her university professor who got Giant Bikes to provide a fleet of bikes for a student tour group that was circum-cycling the island of Taiwan. Though she wasn't used to it, she saw that she had to ask for the help to be considered for sponsorship.

She approached Giant Bikes with a proposal to sponsor her, and the Taiwan-based company was willing to give her a chance, even though it had never sponsored an individual athlete before. The initial contract started with a bike frame. She still had to pay for everything else that went on her bike. As she began to prove her consistent race results, Sally negotiated for bike components to be included in her contract and a monetary bonus for delivering strong race results.

As Sally was placing in the top three at most events and gaining positive media attention, Nike approached her. Every year, Sally would receive compensation in the form of merchandise. There was an incentive for attending Nike events to receive monetary bonuses. Eventually, Sally would get a small salary compensation.

At this time, Sally had two major sponsorships and was also a brand ambassador for Lezyne, a bike accessory brand. As a brand ambassador, Sally was provided with some merchandise and was briefly featured in a Lezyne ad. In 2014, Sally won the Red Bull sponsored event Wings for Life in Taiwan and subsequently received a lifetime supply of Red Bull. She also spent a couple of years at Taiwan's National Training Center, which provided her with housing and accommodations. Ultimately, one of her biggest sponsors was the Taichung National Bank, which acted as a patron to provide some monetary compensation. All this provided just enough support for Sally to race. What started as a need for a working bike frame led Sally to being able to dedicate herself solely to racing.

She retired in 2015, following a decade of racing competitively. Sally never achieved her close-kept childhood dream of becoming an Olympian—she had to reconcile that there was always going to be someone better. Sally notified her sponsors that she would not be renewing her contracts. Looking back, she could've renegotiated the contracts and pitched other value-add than just race results. The business acumen didn't kick in, but the bigger reason may be that Taiwan also didn't have the ecosystem of sports sponsorship outside of professional-level racing and results at the time.

Training is still a crucial part of her routine and she is now affiliated with more recreational teams. In 2018, the largest distributor of Specialized, a bike brand, hired her as a coach and course planner. Sally hopes to develop her coaching career and races for fun now.

The largest step is putting yourself out there. Sally's consistent race results and even her influence in the sports community gave her credibility, but it was her persistence and willingness to put herself out there that landed her sponsors. Racing can be scary because it puts you up against really good athletes, but it also puts you in front of brand sponsors and introduces you to the sport community at large. Submit that application, send that email, make the connections, and don't be afraid to ask. Companies may scope out top performers on their own, but it only hurts to be passive. There is an upside to being well connected and visible through your own efforts.

## THREE

# THE BUSINESS MIND

---

**MONEY, MONEY, MONEY**

Cody Beals, a professional Canadian triathlete appropriately summarizes the necessity for having a business mind:

> *"I've learned a lot about sponsorship over the years. My background is not business. But I quickly realized that to hack it as a professional triathlete, you really really have to be pretty conversant in the language of business and pretty interested in business in order to make it work. For example, last year, even winning those five races, prize money wasn't the biggest line item on my revenue. It was definitely sponsorship. So, it's really, really difficult to earn a living exclusively through sponsorship… the two have to work together. And people will often say, 'You know, it's not all about results. Results don't matter at all.' … In my experience, that's not been the case at all. I would say that certain types of contracts aren't available to athletes without a certain level of results. So, results certainly*

*open doors, but it's other attributes that help close deals.*"[11]

Those other attributes are personality, professionalism, value-add, social media, and so on. Athletes cannot be one-dimensional because it affects their top line. Professional athletes have to be aware of their income and expenses to make sure they have enough funds to compete. For professional triathletes, many of them start with a full-time corporate job and then transition into racing professionally. Some have flexible work schedules that allow them to take their pro card. Others make it work by competing full-time and picking up part-time jobs. Eventually, many make a living solely through race winnings and sponsorships. To get to that level takes a bit of time, as sports can have a high cost associated with racing and competing.

The difference between pros and amateurs in triathlons is that amateur athletes do keep their jobs to fund their sport pursuits. The numbers show the average household income for amateur competing in Ironman is $126,000, based on a study done in 2009.[12] Obviously, making six figures isn't the reality of every athlete competing at the amateur level.

Regardless, between high equipment costs and race entries, sponsorship is filling the gap to help subsidize the cost to compete in a sport.

---

11   Facebook (Wattie Ink, July 11, 2019).

12   "USA Triathlon Demographics," Team USA, accessed November 10, 2019.

Companies are now focusing on building platforms to bridge the connection between those who can provide resources and athletes that need support. Peakz, a company based in the Netherlands, provides a platform for budding athletes to crowdfund support from fans. It is filling a need that there is a deficit of funding to allow athletes to reach the top.[13]

With the tools of the digital age, adopting a business mindset can marry the different parts of the athlete brand/business to help an athlete get sponsorship.

One professional athlete who has really invested in herself as a business is Sonya Looney, an outdoor adventure athlete and American Pro Mountain Biker.

**MARKETING MEDIA COMPANY**
Sonya Looney treats herself as a marketing media company. She made all the jumps in her life by herself. Born and raised in Albuquerque, New Mexico, she eventually went on to win the WEMBO 24 Hour World Championship in 2015.[14] Throughout her career, she put herself next to people she could lean on and surrounded herself with people she aspired to be like. Chasing her "why," along with some flexibility and calculated risks, led her to where she is now. Throughout the years, her biggest battle has been believing in herself.

---

13  "The Funding Problem in Sports," Peakz, December 20, 2019.
14  "Sonya Looney—24h World Champion," Stages Cycling—North America, October 6, 2016.

Growing up, Sonya never identified as an athlete and instead pursued higher education. After graduating with a bachelor of science in electrical engineering from the University of New Mexico in 2005, Sonya moved to Boulder, Colorado, and attended graduate school.

Planting semi-permanent roots in Boulder and leaving the confines of her hometown was a conscious decision to surround herself with people she aspired to be like. The community saw biking as a possible career and didn't think Sonya was chasing a pipe dream. Along with her degree, Sonya started racing competitively after falling in love with mountain biking. In 2006, Sonya raced her first full season as a pro cross country mountain biker while still in school. Looking back, the strong community of people who accepted her dream of having a career as a professional athlete led Sonya to go pro.

> "I didn't have any financial support from family or anything like that," Sonya said. "So, I just—I just took a risk. And, fortunately, it kind of worked out in the end."

Without her family providing financial support, Sonya took on credit card debt to cover her race expenses. She rode a sub-par bike and took hand-me-down clothes to chase her dream.

In 2007, Sonya completed her master's degree in electrical and biomedical engineering and started working at a solar design engineering startup. Her mind, however, was still on mountain biking, so Sonya made a leap of faith. She diverged from her path as an electrical engineering graduate degree with a startup career to pursue her dream.[15]

Around the same time, she started blogging about biking, expecting a handful of acquaintances to read her writing. After going to Sea Otter, the largest outdoor biking event in California, she realized she had somewhat of a following when vendors approached her to write product reviews. Through networking and meeting reps, she also got an offer to race with the Topeak Ergon team. The initial package came with a kit with a top and bottom and some Topeak products, as the company makes bike equipment and accessories. She still had to shell out money for her bike and most race expenses. Sonya funneled the racing and writing to building her personal brand. The company that organized the team liked what Sonya was doing and offered her a national marketing manager role to grow the brand.

She had no prior experience in marketing, but Sonya was very successful gaining exposure for Topeak. Five years in and having grown her brand exposure, she wanted some help with race entry fees. The salary compensation for her work as the national sales and marketing liaison only paid $25,000. This wasn't enough to cover her racing career or any of the student debt she still had. The company declined her request, so she tried taking another avenue. Sonya sent sponsorship

---

15   Sonya Looney, "Meet Sonya," Sonya Looney, accessed January 27, 2020.

proposals to the team's affiliated companies, hoping to get direct financial support. She didn't get any requited interest. Luckily for her, two other brands reached out to her wanting Sonya to represent them. DeFeet, a sock company, and Michael David Winery wanted to collaborate.[16] Because there was no conflict of interests with the current sponsors through the Topeak Ergon team, Sonya jumped on board.

In 2014, Sonya knew it was time for her to make her next move. She left the Topeak Ergon team and, consequently, her marketing job directly tied to the company, noting that between the products and minimal compensation, there wasn't enough to make her stay. With the encouragement of her husband that she could run her own brand, she moved to Canada, where she settled and embarked on running her own business.[17]

Sponsorship proposal after sponsorship proposal, Sonya eventually curated a portfolio that provided more financial support than her previous job. She now has more than fifteen sponsors with brands such as Scott bikes, Kask helmets, and GU nutrition. Her ethos has been, "I think that the key is you have to treat yourself as a business. You are not enough if you aren't a business. You are a media marketing company."

It's a ton of work and, ultimately, Sonya's business comes first. Training is a necessary component; however, it is second in priority to her social media. In the past, the only connection

---

16  Mike Blewitt, "Sonya Looney Leaves Topeak Ergon to Start Her Own Project," MarathonMTB.com, January 6, 2015.

17  Sonya Looney, "Meet Sonya," Sonya Looney, accessed January 27, 2020.

to the audience as a racer was the podium finish; however, with social media, athletes are more and more connected to potential consumers even before hitting the start line.

## CUSTOMER FIRST

Athletes can push products for their sponsors without being the fastest. As long as they are intentional with their brand relationship, they can bring value to whoever they work with. Brian Kennedy, better known for his channel BKXC, also embodies providing value to his community first before trying to be the fastest or the best.

Brian states:

> "I'm pretty much a normal guy. I'm not the fastest [or] slowest guy. I'm not the fittest guy. I'm kind of very much a representative of the common man.... I quit my job. [People] have stuck around and just watch this journey as I've gotten better on the bike.... I think there is a level everyone wants to root for the underdog, root for the protagonist in the story."

Brian saw an opportunity in creating YouTube videos and monetizing through the platform Patreon after being inspired by Nate Hill's Lower Hangover video in Sedona, Arizona.[18] Having some small success reviewing smart sprinkler controls, he created his first videos in 2016, reviewing a bike stand and then a wearable gimbal.

---

18   Brian Kennedy, "The BKXC Origin Story," BKXC (BKXC, July 27, 2016).

Luckily, he entered the YouTube space at an opportune time when there were only a few people making premium biking content. Many videos were shaky or low quality with ambient noise or techno music in the background. Seizing the opportunity, Brian took off from work and dove right in. He started making videos inspired by the format of *Jay Leno's Garage* and Matt Farah's *The Smoking Tire*, where the host added commentary to a mostly pedestrian task.[19] Brian aspired to bring high quality content and great personality to his fans with his simple model of "riding the best trails in the world."

Very quickly, Brian joined Patreon, a platform created by Jack Conte in 2013. This platform allowed fans to directly support creators with monetary subscriptions. This helped budding YouTube creators immensely, because rather than relying on AdSense pennies, creators could get directly compensated for their work. Fans could elect which level of contribution they wanted to give, such as $1, $3, or $10 a month. Creators could have leeway to decide how they want to design their tiers and what perks fans would get at each level of contribution. Common tiers included swag, early access to videos, or live chats. The platform gave fans direct access to creators and leveraged an age-old model where money could fund the arts.

For Brian, it was really scary to reach out to his early viewers for $3 a month, but it ultimately gave him the financial freedom to continue BKXC. To him, getting monthly direct patronage was more impactful than a viewer spending thirty hours watching all his YouTube videos.

---

19   Ibid.

"I knew that it was going to be a very scary thing to go to my fans and say, 'Hey, like, if you want to support me. Three bucks a month.' ... Patreon money is so much more than three bucks a month. It's so much more impact[ful] than someone watching all my videos for a month.... One person watching twenty of my videos in a month might be forty cents or something like that.... So, I had a lot of faith that Patreon would work."

Along the way, Brian discovered the three laws of YouTube—quality, consistency, and personality—to grow his fan base.[20] He also saw artists and other YouTubers take advantage of the Patreon platform.

When Brian joined in 2016, the model was still in the early stages of adoption and critics saw Patreon as e-begging. Patreon gained popularity because creators couldn't survive only on AdSense. Most creators, like Brian, made some money from ad revenue, but Patreon eclipsed the prior way of monetizing. What was crucial for Brian was that Patreon allowed differentiated reward tiers. Brian started with more tiers, but settled on $1, $3, $10, and $25 dollar-a-month tiers. The rewards range from extended and early cuts, to invitation to group rides, to sticker packs and t-shirts.

He found success creating exclusivity around some of the swag. After two months of support, fans would get a sticker pack. At a higher monthly tier, they could get a t-shirt in

---

20  Brian Kennedy, "The Three Laws of YouTube: How I Picked Up 1,000 Subscribers in 100 Days," BKXC (BKXC, July 27, 2016).

an exclusive color. He kept a $50 per month and a $100 per month tier for a bit, but realized he really wasn't getting the return on his time for them.

Brian has forgone the top two tiers because scheduling took too much of his time and the relationships created were too forced. The top tier obligations were also not a reflection of his brand. Instead, he dedicates his focus on putting his fans first, leaning into his excitable and authentic personality. He now releases videos to his core patrons earlier than the Monday, Wednesday, and Friday release to the general YouTube audience. His core fans also receive extended cuts and community perks.

His philosophy and commitment to his audience carries into how he thinks about company sponsorships. When he was starting out, he sent cold emails to represent products and received no responses. As BKXC grew a sizable fan base and crossed the one hundred fifty thousand-subscriber line, suddenly everyone wanted a piece of it. Companies ship him products he doesn't want with the hope he will feature them, but Brian is super cognizant of the impact of taking on or promoting certain products.

> "So, I'm wary of promoting other products.... [I want to keep my] brand authentic and untarnished.... basically protecting my brand up to the point where I feel like okay, now I want to make my own handlebars. I want to make my own pedals and actually sell those and package those and launch them to my audience because that's something I believe in. Versus taking a quick paycheck from a random faceless company

*that says, 'Hey, we want to get our pedals and our handlebars out there. I don't even really know what you do, but here's one hundred bucks. And it looks like you have a lot of followers.' Like I really want to keep with the companies that actually have followed me from the beginning and that are rooting for me and that are really good people."*

He works with brands he trusts such as Hand Up Gloves and Worldwide Cyclery over nameless, faceless brands. Brian also prefers opportunities when he can dictate the partnership, collaborate, and capture more product profits. Through his exposure and fan base, Brian has found a lot of success promoting his merchandise. Teespring.com and hired designers all over the world helped Brian launch BKXC t-shirts. He is wary of working with brands and companies without a pre-established relationship because he can capture more benefits if he maintains creative direction. The partnerships help build up his own brand and grow his business.[21] The fruits of his labor showed when on September 25, 2019, Brian hit three hundred thousand YouTube subscribers around his three-year mark and he continues to maintain a community of one thousand five hundred patrons on Patreon.[22]

Brian understands his audience is first and that the community he created is super important for his channel and business. He wouldn't have grown his audience if there wasn't

---

21 "150,000 Subscriber Update!," YouTube (YouTube, May 25, 2018).
22 "I Quit My Job Three Years Ago and You Kept This Channel Going," YouTube (YouTube, September 27, 2019).

an entrepreneurial mindset to his content and engagement strategy. This is a customer-centric view.

Sonya produces podcasts, writes reviews, and speaks at events to build exposure. Brian understands who his target audience is. Most athletes run an Instagram or social media account to promote their cause. Cody articulates that the business mind needed to hack it provides more upside than being one-dimensional. Amateur athletes may not need to completely live and die by a profit and loss balance sheet, but understanding your niche and value shouldn't be taken lightly.

The business mindset is understanding the financial (not necessarily purely monetary) component of sport sponsorships. What that may mean is investing in parts of the business (yourself) like marketing (personal brand), audience building (social media/network), and income (financial sheet). The business mindset reinforces the other aspects of sport, such as racing and networking, to provide a strong foundation.

FOUR

# A-TEAM ASSEMBLE

Behind every successful athlete is a whole network of support. Professional athletes have the luxury of the best in class coaches, medical professionals, and familial support. Though it may be hard to achieve the same level of support, amateur athletes can create strong support systems to help them achieve their goals. Athletes can do this by both building a team or joining a team to achieve their sponsorship aspirations. This can come in the form of a sponsored team, strong athlete community, or leveraging existing connections to move toward the goal.

**JOIN THE RUSCH**
It's definitely a lot tougher to be an athlete nowadays. Athletes are expected to be a Jack-of-all-trades, really making it hard to be a professional athlete. With Rebecca Rusch's career trajectory, she is now excited to be in a collaborative partnership with her sponsors. It is nice to get a paycheck in the mail, but more exciting to be a part of something.

Rebecca has expanded her reach enormously. She has raised enough funds to clear 99,249 square meters of Unexploded Ordnance (UXO) contamination and raised money for other charities. Rebecca leads camps and runs an annual gravel race called Rebecca's Private Idaho. She has also authored her autobiography *Rusch to Glory* and spoke at TEDxSun-Valley. To handle her many responsibilities, Rebecca needs to dedicate her time to doing things she cannot outsource. She has outsourced her social media and administrative work to her team and funnels her sponsorship money to fund her own business support.

The seven-time world champ "Queen of Pain" Rebecca Rusch built her professional career on the premise of passion. Throughout her three decades of adventure racing, "enduro" mountain bike competitions, and crazy expedition feats, she has defined what she really stands for. For Rebecca, it has been about respect and building a strong team to support her. This has pushed her to part with her twelve-year sponsorship with Specialized Bicycles, one of the largest bike brands in the industry, because the company never understood her as an athlete and because she moved toward expedition riding rather than pure racing.[23]

Leaving a sponsor was a tough decision, because Rebecca internalized the breakup as a reflection of her failure to effect change. But, year after year, Rebecca had to defend her athletic legitimacy with Specialized. She was tired of the one-year contracts and the feeling that the company didn't

---

23  Bike, "Rebecca Rusch Partners with Niner Bikes," BIKE Magazine (BIKE Magazine, January 21, 2015).

understand her. Whether she knew it at the time or not, she needed people who would be a part of her success team, not add more stress and set back her goals. The decade-plus relationship that Rebecca developed just wasn't working, but it was still emotional to walk away.

Taking a closer look, the fallout elevated Rebecca's other sponsorship relationships. It forced her to reevaluate what it meant to be Rebecca Rusch as she dialed in on working with companies that fit who she was. She signed with Niner Bikes from 2015 to 2019, a smaller bike brand that specializes in 29er (size of the wheel) mountain bikes.[24] In 2020, Rebecca announced her new partnership with Liv and Giant Bikes.[25] Other brands signed up to be a part of what Rebecca represented and joined the team. Garmin, a sports technology company, took notice and was willing to invest more resources when convinced of Rebecca's commitment to the female adventure racing space. There were other sponsorship matches like Assos, a Swiss apparel company, that approached Rebecca Rusch wanting to create more female-oriented apparel. In conjunction, Red Bull, Rebecca's more than seventeen-year-long steadfast sponsor, continued to provide project-based opportunities outside of her athlete contract.

Rebecca relied on her team of sponsors to be able to achieve ambitious goals. It took her years of pitching an idea, being

---

24  Mike Cushionbury, "Endurance Legend Rebecca Rusch Signs with Niner Bikes • Dirt Rag," Dirt Rag, January 21, 2015.

25  "Liv and Giant USA Announce Partnership with Rebecca Rusch," YouTube (YouTube, January 22, 2020).

rejected, refining her proposal, and pitching again before Red Bull finally gave her the manpower for the project she had in mind. She knew she needed the support of a strong crew behind her to tell the story she wanted to.

In 2017, Rebecca embarked on biking the full 1,200-mile length of the Ho Chi Minh trail, documented in the film *Blood Road*. Rebecca was in search of the crash site where her late father's fighter pilot plane got shot down during the Vietnam war forty years earlier. Armed with Red Bull Media's production support, Niner bike's mechanic, local guides, and sheer will, Rebecca and her Vietnamese counterpart traversed through Vietnam, Cambodia, and Laos on the Unexploded Ordnance—or unexploded bomb—laced trail. The route went through Southeast Asia in a land still affected by the aftermath of the Vietnam War.

She was kept in the dark for the planning and struggled with not having any control over the project she worked so hard to make happen.[26] The Red Bull Media Director orchestrated the routes and filming. The crew and subjects struggled to gel at the beginning of the project, and it wasn't until Rebecca learned to let go of her desire to dictate everything and wanting to control the artistic direction of the story did the team chemistry improve. It took a village to make her journey successful. In the end, Rebecca's trust in the team got her further than she could've imagined and crafted a very poignant film of her journey.

---

26  "Letting Go, Slowing Down and Trusting Others: Rebecca Rusch Reflects on the Making of Blood Road," Niner Bikes, July 18, 2017.

Rebecca relies on a strong team to get her to where she needs to be. Delegating the social media, scheduling, and coordinating responsibilities allows her to focus on her impact on the world. Learning to rely on creative and filming directive from an industry person helped Rusch invoke the audience response parallel to the emotional journey she went on. Everything Rebecca does wouldn't have happened without her team.

## T-E-A-M

Rebecca still pulls together people who support her vision. Elite amateur athletes can similarly be intentional about who they surround themselves with to build their success team.

Maybe social media or personal brand building isn't your strong suit. Leverage friends, family, or other athletes in the community to help you. Maybe you need to divest some of the time you do in administrative work and invest it in your sports instead. It may help to hire a coach or consult an expert in the field. Maybe your friends and family are kind enough to step in and help plan logistics when you race or compete. These are all people that will unconditionally support your sport to help you race, build your personal brand, and give you more ammo to apply for that sponsored team or start that conversation with a brand.

In my athletic journey, my mother has been my number one support in my triathlon endeavors. No matter where in the world I travel, she is right there with me, spending hours outside to spectate a race. Leading up to my biggest and last race of 2019, my mother had already spectated and supported three full Ironman distance races. This included traveling to locations all over the world like Penghu, Taiwan; Taupo, New Zealand; and Cairns, Australia. This doesn't even begin to go into the requirements of being a spectator during race day. This entails being outside for twelve-plus hours, much of the time having to be wary of not only tracking me on the course, but also not neglecting necessities like eating, staying hydrated, and so on. This is the type of support I'm grateful for, and it allows me to race and give back to the team and brands that sponsor me. My mother is absolutely core to my success team.

How you craft your winning team can create a self-fulfilling cycle to help you gain more support and open more doors.

**KIRSTEN KASPER**
Intentionally building the so-called team can also work in tandem with joining a team. Again, all of this is to create a positive feedback loop.

Let's take a look at how Kirsten Kasper, a USA short-course professional triathlete, leverages the team she joined along with her self-selected team to help her with sponsorships.

Kirsten Kasper ran track and field and cross country at Georgetown University. She did relatively well, but definitely did not have a blowout career in just running. In 2012, she finished sixth and seventh in the 3,000 m and the 5,000 m, respectively, in the Big East Conference Tournament. During that same year, her senior year, she finished twelfth in the

Canadian Olympic Trials for the 1,500 m.[27] Her Olympic dreams didn't end there. Kirsten stayed for her master's and ended up running a fifth year at her alma mater. The Blue and Gray program was very high caliber and the level of training and commitment needed to be a part of that team prepared Kirsten well for being a professional athlete.

With her collegiate running career and a background in swimming from adolescence, she got into triathlons because of the USA Triathlon's recruitment program. In June of 2014, she traveled to California to try out in front of USAT coaches. They believed in her potential, brought her into the program, and taught her how to ride competitively. The program was fully funded with its own sponsors. Kirsten received her initial bike and wetsuit from the established network.

In 2017 and 2018, she was consistently ranked fourth in the World Triathlon Series (WTS). Four years after going through the USA Triathlon training program and getting consistent race results, Kirsten on-boarded an agent associated with the Santara Group, a talent management and brand marketing agency.[28] Her agent works in tandem with Kirsten's athletic aspirations. The acts of delivering results and getting financial support reinforce one another for a professional athlete.

Kirsten needs the backing to keep training and needs the results to get the sponsorships. This is Kirsten's own business

---

27   "2013-14 Women's XC/Track Roster," Georgetown University Athletics, accessed November 15, 2019.

28   "Kirsten Kasper," Santara Group, accessed November 15, 2019.

team, and her agent has continued to build off Kirsten's initial connections. Her Oakley sponsorship came from meeting the rep and her ROKA sponsorship came from her coach. ROKA started sponsoring her during her debut year after she only raced three events. Her agent manages closing deals and negotiating Kirsten's contracts. Kirsten still dictates her sponsorship flow but has more time to focus on her social media presence, racing, and her dream of Olympic qualification.

Results wise, Kirsten continues to train and race in the WTS circuit while getting invites, courtesy of her agent, from more prestigious triathlon events such as Super League and Island House Triathlon. These races allow Kirsten to continue to prove herself and grow as an athlete. Kirsten aims to be authentic and supportive of the brands that have been loyal to her and the brands' financial support allows Kirsten to continue her qualification bid for the Tokyo 2020 Olympic Games.

The first chance to qualify for Kirsten was at the ITU World Olympic qualification event in Tokyo in August 2019. In a crazy turn of events, first- and second-place finishers Jessica Learmonth and Georgia Taylor-Brown from Team Great Britain were disqualified for crossing the tape holding hands in celebration, violating ITU rule 2.11 "Athletes who finish in a contrived tie situation, where no effort to separate their finish times has been made, will be DSQ."[29] This defaulted

---

29 "Summer Rappaport Qualifies For 2020 Tokyo Olympic Games," Triathlete, (Triathlete, August 15, 2019).

the win to world champion Flora Duffy, a Bermudan athlete, in her comeback season after a foot injury.[30]

During the race, Teresa Zaferes, who has shared many a podium with her Team USA teammate Kirsten, crashed into Kirsten Kasper on the bike. This took Zaferes, arguably the top USA female contender, out of the race. Based on USA Olympic selection rules, with no podium finishers, one Olympic slot is allocated to the first in the top eight finishers, which was Summer Rappaport, who finished in fifth place and earned her Olympic bid.[31]

Going into 2020, one USA Olympic slot has already been allocated, leaving one slot left. Kirsten has another chance to qualify for the Tokyo 2020 games in May 2020 at the ITU World Triathlon Series in Yokohama, Japan. She would need to podium as one of the fastest USA female athletes or finish as the fastest top eight women to secure her spot. No matter how it plays out, Kirsten's team is crucial to her success as a professional athlete with Olympic aspirations.

Having a team helps distribute work, makes people happier, and can engender more creative ideas. With honest feedback, mutual respect, and personal openness, members are 80

---

[30] Beau Dure and Associated Press, "Summer Rappaport Clinches Olympic Triathlon Berth in Tumultuous Qualifier—OlympicTalk: NBC Sports," OlympicTalk | NBC Sports, August 15, 2019.

[31] "Summer Rappaport Qualifies For 2020 Tokyo Olympic Games," Triathlete, (Triathlete, August 15, 2019).

percent more likely to report higher emotional well-being.[32] Studies have proven the key role that parents play to alleviate emotional distress and provide support for elite athletes.[33] Figuring out the people who are part of your success team and perhaps joining a team in tandem creates a virtuous cycle enabling you to lean on a network for support. This allows you to demonstrate, through racing and competing, your value to existing and potential sponsors.

---

32  Tracy Middleton, "The Importance of Teamwork (as Proven by Science)," Work Life by Atlassian (Atlassian, December 20, 2019).

33  Joseph Baker et al., "Nurturing Sport Expertise: Factors Influencing the Development of Elite Athlete," Journal of sports science & medicine (Asist Group, March 1, 2003).

FIVE

# IT'S A SMALL, SMALL WORLD

## SPORTS INDUSTRY

The sports industry is small for both brands and athletes alike. To be successful at attaining sports sponsorships, it helps to understand the network effect and also the community dynamics. A sponsored athlete can help maintain a brand's culture by bringing in other athletes that align with the brand's sponsorship program. Sponsored opportunities can also arise based on "who you know." The industry is small enough that brands have incentive to preserve their intellectual property rights. But, going after other brands within the industry can sour public brand image of the aggressor. Ultimately, athletes and brands both play their part in reinforcing the established community.

## LULU COMMUNITY

Lululemon, the pioneer of the athleisure category of the fitness clothing market, used the connections of its brand ambassadors in two ways to build up their brand. First, sponsored Lululemon ambassadors would recommend other ambassadors based on their own networks. It's easier for the brand to understand what value the sponsored party would bring if a prospective recruit has already been screened by the sponsored party's network or already has an established reputation. Second, the company strategy guaranteed exposure for the Lululemon brand by tapping into the teacher-student relationship. From the start, ambassadors taught or led free classes in exchange for Lululemon products. Ambassadorships usually started with an already acquainted relationship to the local shop and continued to grow as new ambassadors brought their connections into the Lululemon fold.

Lauren Padula Neroni and Angelo Neroni's involvement with Lululemon's ambassadorship stemmed from their connection to the La Jolla store. Lauren, a physical therapist and yoga instructor, and Angelo, a runner and fitness enthusiast didn't speak about their Lululemon ambassadorship as anything super extraordinary. Lauren became friends with the Lululemon run ambassador at the La Jolla store when she started the San Diego chapter of November Project, a free fitness movement, in 2014. To grow the meet ups, she connected with as many people in the running community as possible. Her Lululemon predecessor was finishing up her ambassadorship and referred Lauren as the next store-run ambassador. At the time, Lauren had no idea what the two-year ambassadorship meant. She knew she would get free clothes and have her photo in store banners in exchange for leading workouts. Her first year was mainly acclimating and it wasn't until her second year that she was introduced to everything Lululemon could provide.

During her second year, Lauren thought it was a good opportunity to get involved as a pacer in the SeaWheeze Half Marathon that Lululemon organizes every year. Angelo also became a Lululemon run ambassador in 2015. Because of both Lauren and Angelo's involvement with November Project, they were invited to the Lululemon Ambassador Summit to meet other ambassadors. Both Lauren and Angelo became pretty involved in the Lululemon community. They ended up becoming contributors to a fitness blog that another Lululemon ambassador was maintaining and they led a workout for a five hundred-store manager retreat on another occasion. Their flights and accommodations were covered and they were really psyched to share their workouts with the larger Lululemon community. Angelo did some modeling and also participated in product development for the brand. Through the two-year run ambassador rotation, they got to meet a lot of people and took advantage of various opportunities.

In the case of Lauren and Angelo, they were involved in the Lululemon community prior to their ambassadorships and were able to connect with more fitness enthusiasts. They brought more people into the Lululemon fold and Lululemon also provided opportunities for them to give back. The Lululemon network is built on all of these prior connections.

Another take away is it helps to get an "in" in the community that you would like to be a part of prior to even thinking about sponsorship. If you would like a Lululemon ambassadorship, are you involved in the local meetup community? Do you know people at the local retail store? Do you already give back to the community or have an influence you can offer?

Lululemon isn't the only environment where this is important. Take Wattie Ink for example. Prior to applying to Wattie Ink's team, I was doing what I could to represent the brand at different races. On the course, I would respond to people shouting "Rock the W" or the generic Wattie cheers.

Because the sport sponsorship world is small, actively strategizing how to be a part of the community prior to being sponsored increases the chance of getting an "in." It not only provides an idea of what the community support system is like, but it also provides those with decision-making power an idea of who you would be as a brand representative.

**LAUREN GREGG**
Lauren Gregg's story is another example of how small the sports community is. In fact, it is so small that Lauren Gregg is a champion of non-endemic sports sponsorship when monetary resourcing is scarce within the industry. She is a former cross country pro mountain biker who harps on the importance of the community. Over the decade of riding, Lauren has figured out three things:

1. Build the relationship
   Much of the biking world is who you know. Once you establish credibility with one manager, they can usually recommend you to another, but it also depends on the person you work with. Some of Lauren's sponsors came after grabbing beers.
2. Know the target audience of the company
   As a woman, Lauren positioned herself to identify with 50 percent of the population, targeting the XX chromosome

buyers. She noted that most male riders had already decided their brand loyalties, whereas female riders getting into the sport had yet to commit to a brand.
3. Do the heavy lifting
   Earlier in Lauren's career, she thought if she positioned herself as willing and able, a company would be open to collaborate. It took Lauren a while to realize that companies initially want to do as little work as possible. The odds are higher for the company to show the money if the answer is a binary yes or no.

Lauren had artistic aspirations when she was younger and never saw sports as her career. To her parents' relief, she never became a starving musician but, funnily enough, she did choose to be a houseless (not homeless) nomadic biker living out of her XL 250 Ford Transit, endearingly named Loosy. Put in her own words, convincing Ford to give her a sprinter van was a Hail Mary, as she had to make a convincing case as to why Ford should sponsor her with a sprinter van.

To do so, Lauren created a deck exposing that Ford's competitors, Dodge and Mercedes, had brand representation in built out sprinter vans, whereas Ford didn't. To make her case, Lauren offered to design and construct a livable space within Ford's sprinter van and live in it for at least a year. She handed over her schedule of races, promising Ford exposure through her travels. She found a random email address of one of Ford's marketing managers, crossed her fingers, and sent her proposal off. To Lauren's surprise, the contract came with the van and some monetary subsidy.

In 2016, Lauren designed and built her custom Ford camper and lived in her van full time for two-and-a-half years. She designed the bed to be lofted toward the rear of the van with a passenger seat and cabinets in the midsection. Storage was set to be tucked away in the sides and additional storage was designed under the seat. From the dual rear doors to the trunk, or functionally the garage, a couple bikes could fit in the van without much disassembly. The van was also outfitted with solar panels and a simple HVAC system for temperature control.[34]

Lauren, self-described as a creative artist and musician, fell into the biking world upon taking her dad's old mountain bike out for a ride, inspired by the movie *The Collective*, which documents mountain bikers going out and riding. In the early 2000s, Lauren was ambivalent about her artistic endeavors; making it in the female racing world seemed like the appropriate next challenge. The industry was not welcoming to female mountain bikers at the time. Female riders weren't taken seriously and the events were seen as hobbyists partaking in a side show to the main male competition.

During that time, there was little sponsorship to go around in the male field, and given the sentiment about female bikers, there was even less sponsorship allocated for female riders. Lauren spent the first five years piecing together small sums of money from disparate companies to cover her expenses. Her annual spreadsheet laid out exactly how much sponsorship money she needed to cover gas, race fees, and, if she

---

34  "Lauren Gregg's Custom Ford Transit Van," Pinkbike, (Pinkbike, May 19, 2016).

was lucky, her living necessities. It was a seasonal lifestyle where her credit card debt would pile up during the racing season and Lauren would then work various jobs during the winter to pay off her debts. Leveraging the preestablished relationships, she would sometimes fill open positions at the companies that sponsored her.

Before 2014, Bear Valley Bikes was her debut team and her first sponsor. She received her bike frame, nutrition, kit, and so on through the team's affiliates. She also worked at Specialized Bicycle Components for a year. Around this time, Lauren was starting to feel the grind of submitting race resumes each year, trying to make the season and training work, and receiving rejections in turn.

As a result, Lauren decided to switch biking disciplines from cross country to enduro. Cross Country riders competed for the faster time along a mountain biking course whereas enduro riders competed for combined times over three to five downhill stages of a course. The timing coincided with increasing popularity of the less cardio intensive enduro format.

At one of her first enduro events at Sea Otter, Lauren was offered a Fox sponsorship over beers. She thought the rep was just drunk and wouldn't remember the interaction, but Lauren wanted the sponsorship and was unsure of how she should follow up. At her next race, the Fox rep came up to her and asked her what she was doing on her old bike, confirming that she was a Fox athlete now. It was the first big break for Lauren and it granted her the affirmation and confidence she needed going forward; there were even tears involved. From there, the connection with Fox opened doors to companies like Yeti, Scratch Labs, Pivot Cycles, and then Fuji Bikes.

Her enduro racing results never quite reached those of her time in cross country racing; however, Lauren found more success in the later part of her career. By then, the industry had shifted perspective and Lauren had years of experience partnering with sponsors. In 2018, she took a marketing manager job with Fuji, one of her latest bike sponsors.

Looking back at her racing career, Lauren realized just how small the mountain biking world is. She got her first big break over beers and got introduced to other brand reps through her current brand managers. Lauren Gregg still champions non-endemic sponsorships because one of her biggest sponsors was Ford, which supplied her with her sprinter van.

It's not surprising that some sponsorship opportunities come from a connection of another connection. In sports sponsorship, it pays to have a good grasp of the network, but it also pays to be a little creative if there are no obvious leads. Lauren was successful in pitching to a non-sport brand that she could bring value to. For an elite amateur athlete, building strong connections within the industry will never hurt. Who knows? Maybe a little creativity on top of that network will open up untapped opportunities.

### HOW SPECIALIZED?

The sports community is small and resources aren't limitless. Brands want the best people to represent them and have a huge incentive to differentiate themselves and preserve what makes them unique. The margins that big bicycle companies operate within incentivizes them to be extremely protective of their brand, almost picking petty fights for a competitive advantage.

"It's the battle of the symbols ®, ©, and ™," as Derrick Lewis, a former industry marketing manager, put it. He spent a couple decades engaging consumers for brands like Rapha and Specialized Bicycle Component. It was a joke that ran in the industry, as cycling companies rushed to copyright, trademark, and register what they claim as their intellectual property (IP) rights.

The brand most notorious for having an iron fist over IP rights is Specialized Bicycle Component. Specialized strives to make the best products—not just great products, but the absolute best products. To protect its research and development, the Specialized legal team has been infamously known to flex its legal power in IP disputes.

In 1990, Specialized sued RockShox Inc. for the resemblance to Rockhopper. In 2006, the company sued Mountain Cycle's use of the word Stumptown, which Specialized claimed was too similar to Stumpjumper. Specialized also had a trademark dispute with Revelate Designs, known as Epic Designs at the time, over bag designs in 2009. In 2012, Specialized went on what amounted to a witch hunt against two former employees for establishing a biking company named Volagi after leaving the biking behemoth. Specialized spent $2.5 million in legal fees on the Volagi case only to lose on all but one count, for which Volagi had to compensate Specialized for $1 worth of damages. In 2013, Specialized might have crossed the line when the company went after a bike shop named Roubaix for using the same name as a Specialized road bike model. The ordeal caused a massive social media backlash.[35] Needless to say, people in the community noticed.

Specialized has definitely flexed its IP rights. It makes a little more sense that Specialized would go to such extremes to maintain control of the brand and its associations since the brand relies on the best components and industry superiority as a differentiator. Specialized may be the worst offender, but there are many other instances of intellectual property lawsuits or threats of litigation that give Specialized a run for its money.

Within the industry, legal battles over naming rights are very common. In 2018, Faraday Bicycles, an electric bike company, sued Faraday Future, an electric car company, over the name.[36] In 2017, a company claiming control of the late comedian Chris Farley's last name, filed $10 million lawsuit against Trek Bicycles over the bike model Farley.[37] My personal favorite is Santa Cruz Bicycles' bike name change in September of 2013, which can only be speculated to have something to do with the drink paraphernalia the red solo cup or another bicycle name. Santa Cruz's public statement claimed:

---

35 "Now You Know," Drunkcyclist.com, (Drunkcyclist.com, March 12, 2014).
36 Ryan Felton, "Faraday Future Is Even Getting Sued by a Bicycle Company," Jalopnik (Jalopnik, April 26, 2017).
37 Steve Frothingham, "Trek Sued Over Use of the Farley Name on Fat Bikes," Bicycle Retailer and Industry News, September 15, 2017.

> *"Some of you may have noticed that … SOLO … has recently been rechristened to … 5010.*
>
> *The rebadging exercise ensures this model can no longer be confused with any other similarly trademarked item … be it a drink cup, a Star Wars character, a Hungarian hybrid car (look it up)[38] or even a 700c rigid bicycle for that matter.*
>
> *So why 5010?*
>
> *If it wasn't already obvious, our product manager is a big fan of NGC 5010, a lenticular galaxy located about 140 million light years away.*
>
> *Why "Go Solo" when you can "Go Intergalactic." Take it away boys …"[39]*

The list goes on, but back to Specialized. Does this absolve Specialized of its arguably petty tactics? Most likely not. Specialized's reputation of lawsuits precedes the company. But there must be a method to the madness. It may be counterintuitive and create a PR issue, but the flip side is that brand protectionism allows Specialized to continue to invest in the best products, inextricably tied to the brand name.

---

38  "Super Hybrid Cars," TrendHunter.com (TREND HUNTER Inc., June 26, 2008).

39  "Solo Becomes 5010," Santa Cruz Bicycles (Santa Cruz Bicycles, September 24, 2014).

With the best products, Specialized has signed some of the best athletes across multiple disciplines. The promise of great products and top industry people attract the best of the best athletes to sign on. Specialized's core brand identity is contingent on making the best products. Making the best products brings in the best people, and the world champions challenge the company to produce better products. The product, brand, and people create a positive feedback loop.

Just as the best brands want to have the best athletes. The best athletes want to represent the best brands. A caveat exists, though. If a brand's ideology fundamentally diverges from what an athlete believes in, it is really hard to create a functioning partnership. Athlete-brand ideology alignment is core to the function of a brand ambassador program. For example, Specialized strives to be the best, so it strives to sign on the best of the best athletes. The sports drink company Nuun encourages egalitarian entry into sports. Rapha evokes emotion and creates the allure of cycling. Lululemon believes in the strength of social groups, therefore, it encourages its ambassadors to create communities.

At the end of the day, Specialized is a performance company. The company wants to be the industry leader for bikes, accessories, and the last frontier for the average sports consumer. Specialized "360 approach" spans everywhere. Specialized has partnered with Zwift and invested in sports tech. Specialized needs the best engineers, designers, marketers, and so on to continue to produce at this caliber.

This ethos has also seeped into the culture of sponsored Specialized athletes. Specialized has been known to bring in new blood, often at the expense of athlete sponsorship tenures. Athlete contracts were only one-year contracts for a long time. Athletes had to defend their legitimacy every year. Gwen Jorgensen's four-year contract covering the period of her pregnancy was extremely unprecedented. A handful of athletes have walked away from the Specialized contract.

Athletes have been held to a high standard, but have also had access to best in class support crew. Specialized's competitive advantage is having the best products to attract the best talent. Within the talent pools, athletes self-organize into clichés based on their disciplines. New sponsored athletes are brought into high performing teams. The short course athletes stick together and the long course athletes find camaraderie.

The verdict of Specialized's impact on the community isn't black or white. Specialized may aggressively protect its own brand and trademarks at the expense of the larger sports industry, but it can also create an environment to build strong networks between its professional (and amateur) athletes. With how small the sports community is, athletes have the ultimate say in whether they want to partner with a brand.

Network patterns build the connections for sponsorship relationships. Brand ambassador programs or team sponsorships rely on word of mouth for athletes to refer other athletes. Brands investing in sponsorship place importance on an athlete's existing network and rely on referrals to preserve their brand's culture. Inherent communities can exist, but it pays for an athlete to invest and facilitate genuine connections. The exact definition of "community" for each athlete is up for interpretation, but nevertheless it's a small, small world.

SIX

# BRAND AMBASSADORS AS AMPLIFIERS

Brands sponsor ambassadors because athletes can help signal what the brand means to the target customers. To help their top line, brands want to capture more of the market, and, if successful, shift consumer demand.

Based on Bain's *Brand Strategy That Shifts Demand*, effective strategy can be broken down into four steps.[40]

1. Define brand meaning
2. Transmit brand message
3. Amplified and/or distorted
4. Adapt to how the brand is received and interacted with

A company first needs to define what its brand stands for, then communicate the brand image to its customers. Once that

---

40  Eric Almquist and Tamar Dane Dor-Ner, "Brand Strategy That Shifts Demand: Less Buzz, More Economics," Bain, November 14, 2014.

brand image is out in the world, the brand impression can be distorted or amplified. Customers can form opinions about the brand. This opens two-sided communication between the company and the customers. Brand ambassadors fit into the third step of this model through brand amplification or distortion. Having a legion of brand promoters can generate positive impressions to the targeted customers. Brands need athletes just as much as athletes may need them to subsidize sports costs.

**THE LULU METHOD**
Lululemon is the model example of creating promoters that amplify the brand to then help the business.

Lululemon started its legion by selecting ambassadors with community influence. The website tagline is "Our athlete programs support a community of driven athletes and inspirational people who harness their passion to elevate their communities."[41]

With thousands of Lululemon ambassadors worldwide, Lululemon started by bringing in yoga instructors that had community influence. Early ambassador structure had Lululemon classes hosted in yoga studios. Then, the company brought classes into the retail space and switched to driving foot traffic into stores. The gatherings also branched out to running, parkour, and so on, along with yoga. Running ambassadors and yoga ambassadors became commonplace, but each retail store had autonomy to decide how they wanted to leverage

---
41  "Ambassadors," Lululemon, accessed December 20, 2019.

Lululemon ambassadors. For example, the local Upper West Side Lululemon that I was a part of wanted to drive male customer traffic, so they offered the ambassadorship to a local Flywheel instructor and triathlon aficionado, Brian Levine. He was offered a Lululemon allowance to buy male clothing and give them out to testers to collect feedback and introduce men to the brand. Similarly, Lauren and Angelo from Chapter 4 were tapped to be Lululemon ambassadors when they were living in San Diego as the La Jolla store wanted ambassadors with influence in the community.

As of 2016, the Lululemon hierarchy of ambassador was made up of a total of eight global yoga ambassadors, seventy-five elite ambassadors, and over one thousand five hundred store ambassadors. For the top tier ambassadors, Lululemon supported organizations such as Vinyasa Yoga for the Youth or Love Your Brain.[42] Lululemon positioned the company to help the ambassadors achieve their goals and the ambassadors spread the gospel.

Today, Lululemon heavily relies on brand ambassadors to amplify what Lululemon stands for. Lululemon's success has been unparalleled and many brands leverage and try to replicate those same grassroot movements to grow brand buy-in.

**SHIFT CUSTOMER DEMAND**
Using brand ambassadors as amplifiers is one part of the marketing funnel to get more potential customers to hear

---

42   Chantal Fernandez, "Inside Lululemon's Unconventional Influencer Network," Fashionista, November 2, 2016.

about the brand. It is one way for brands to promote and market with the goal of attaining heightened brand recognition, which can translate into consumer spending. The end goal of capturing top line dollars is more important than just generating buzz about the brand. Bain's 2015 report argues that brand strategy is more economics than spectacle, saying,

> "That's because the ultimate point of a brand is not to create emotional appeal or to generate buzz. The point is to shift customer demand."[43]

Yes, Lululemon has generated aspirational appeal with the company's market segmentation and fictional muses "Ocean" and "Duke"—Ocean being an active thirty-two-year-old who works out every day and makes six figures, while Duke is a thirty-five-year-old "athletic opportunist" whose interests include snowboarding, surfing, and so on.[44] The muses engendering some type of longing could be argued as emotional appeal, but it's only part of the equation.

The archetype is in part responsible for Lululemon being the go-to athletic brand for many women. What truly made

---

43  Eric Almquist and Tamar Dane Dor-Ner, "Brand Strategy That Shifts Demand: Less Buzz, More Economics," Bain, November 14, 2014.

44  Ashley Lutz, "Lululemon Calls Its Ideal Customers 'Ocean' and 'Duke'—Here's Everything We Know about Them," Business Insider (Business Insider, February 2, 2015).

Lululemon successful was shifting customer demand by creating a completely new shopping category called "athleisure."

Having captured most of the population, Lululemon then shifted to other market segmentation. From Lauren's experience, she witnessed Lululemon's shift from leaning toward community involvement to the lifestyle brand image. Angelo also felt that Lululemon was trying to diversify the types of sport practices it covered. Granted, this was after Lululemon already reached a threshold of influence and had devoted yoga-pants wearing female, and now male, customers.

In 2017, Lululemon did its first large marketing campaign outside of its grassroots model, playing off the conception of "This is Yoga."[45] Lululemon traditionally invested in three main sources of marketing: the retail store, social media, and the website, but seemed like there were more opportunities for Lululemon to branch out.

To move from grassroots to traditional marketing wasn't cheap. This was the most expensive campaign Lululemon had created to date, which broke away from its grassroots origins. This was natural industry progression, as athleisure wasn't an unknown, nascent fashion category anymore. For highly competitive industries like beverages or athletic wear, competition "devolves to an expensive arms race." In industries where most of the giant leaps of innovation have already been made, the only market advantage becomes focusing

---

45   Adrianne Pasquarelli, "Why There's No Yoga in Lululemon's First Global Campaign," Ad Age, May 15, 2017.

marketing and spending into brand promotion and strategizing to gain more market share.

Lululemon did the work to identify and create an untapped category. As first movers, it was successful in shifting customer demand. This paved the way for incumbent fitness brands to jump on the bandwagon, which then shifted the market paradigm.

Lululemon's success came from commanding higher prices and having a legion of fervent brand ambassadors. In Bain's report, there are two ways to shift customer demand: by commanding a higher price point for their products or achieving economies of scale. It is a balancing act between the two levers, as too high a price point will drive away demand and too low a demand will cut into the business's bottom line. What really helped Lululemon maintain a high level of customer confidence even with high price points was a strong brand image. The brand promoters played a part to strengthen the brand image. With a strong brand, the company could push this "intersection of volume and price in order to maximize revenues and profits."

**LAUNCH OFF LIKE A KANGAROO**
Quintana Roo (QR), a subsidiary of American Bicycle Group, also found value in having brand promoters. The brand wanted to compete with the likes of big Ironman World Championship race bicycle players like Cervelo and Canyon and were incentivized to increase the brand presence. The brand saw an opportunity to work with Wattie Ink and

pursue a possible collaboration with the combined 600+ Wattie Ink sponsored athletes.

In 2019, after American Pro Triathlete Heather Jackson three-peated her win in Ironman Chattanooga 70.3, she and Sean "Wattie" Watkins, both cofounders of Wattie Ink, a triathlon clothing brand, toured the American Bicycle Group factory.

A simple signage reading "American Bicycle Group" marks a corrugated metal building in Chattanooga, Tennessee. The 40,000 square foot factory is right off the Ironman Chattanooga course, a space the American Bicycle Group moved to in 2016.[46] Right on South Creek Road, the facility includes a showroom with bikes lining the demo space. On the factory floor, large machinery, operating stations, and lots and lots of bike pieces are strewn about. Off to one part of the factory, the corporate cubicles showcase just a few jerseys of past champions on the office walls.[47]

American Bicycle Group CEO, Peter Hurley, found a really natural partnership opportunity between Wattie Ink, a triathlon apparel company, and Quintana Roo, the triathlon bike brand of American Bicycle Group. There was an opportunity to really lean into something that both brands saw as their core identity, which was Made in America. Peter Hurley pitched what Quintana Roo was capable of offering to Wattie Ink.

---

46  "American Bicycle Group Moves to Larger Facility," Bicycle Retailer and Industry News, August 9, 2016.

47  Zach Overholt, "Factory Tour: Litespeed Celebrates 30 Years of Cutting Edge Titanium Bicycle Manufacturing," Bikerumor, February 19, 2016.

There was a hurdle though, as Heather Jackson was sponsored by Argon 18, a Canadian bike brand. The amateur Elite team, Team Wattie Ink, was too. These were clearly conflicting interests as an athlete cannot race on, and therefore cannot represent, two different bike brands.

But, the Argon 18 and Team Wattie Ink partnership seemed to be shifting. The sponsorship was an inherited relationship carried over from previous management. Back then, Team Wattie Ink was smaller, and as the team grew, it was difficult for Argon 18 to distribute to large team spread across geography. Argon 18 provided affiliate team discounts on bikes during the partnership. From what Peter Hurley was pitching, there was more that the Quintana Roo partnership could offer Team Wattie Ink and, in turn, the group of elite amateur triathletes could also grow the Quintana Roo brand.

Early talks included ideas on how to leverage the elite team and also proposals like custom frame paint jobs. Ironman World Championship qualifiers could earn a QR bike frame to race on in Hawaii. I happened to qualify for Ironman World Championship, or Kona, in 2019 and opted to take the sponsored frame and uphold my end of the sponsorship contract. Quintana Roo really exhibited its level of service as the process for receiving my frame was personal and seamless. I received my brand-new carbon frame within a week of ordering. I was also hyper-cognizant of providing value to Quintana Roo. Although I was only contractually obligated to race Kona on the bike, I also raced my tune-up race Ironman Santa Cruz 70.3 on the Quintana Roo bike and podiumed fourth in my age group. I also contributed to their content about my "Road to Kona," posted on social media, and promoted their agenda for brand presence.

My story is just one of many which Quintana Roo hoped to get out of the partnership. As Peter Hurley and Sean "Wattie" Watkins mentioned in their press release, "This is a natural partnership and one we expect to grow in the future."[48]

QR had an opportunity to not only increase brand presence in the biggest Ironman race of the year, but also could have shifted customer demand within the Wattie Ink ambassadors, as well as other athletes that saw representation in Kona. This could have only been achieved by tapping into athletes who would promote the QR brand. Wattie Ink wasn't the only team that QR provided sponsored bikes to, but it did help that Wattie Ink had the most athletes racing in the Ironman World Championship and a handful of athletes who opted into the bike sponsorship.[49] In return, QR inched toward their brand strategy goals.

**MOVE ZWIFT-LY**
With Lululemon and Quintana Roo, they have invested in athletes to help amplify the brand messaging. Businesses not only leverage brand ambassadors to push a brand's positioning but can also further propel the message when the

---

[48] "Quintana Roo and Wattie Ink Enter into Tri Team Partnership," Endurancebusiness.com, (Endurancebusiness.com, June 4, 2019).

[49] "IRONMAN TriClub Program—Americas," Wattie Ink. had the most members racing…—IRONMAN TriClub Program—Americas, October 29, 2019.

brands inherit some of the ambassadors' existing influence by default.

In 2018, Zwift and Specialized teamed up to offer four slots in the debut of the Specialized Zwift Academy Tri Team. The goal was to create the best supported amateur triathlon team on the planet. Four amateur athletes—Rachael Norfleet, Golo Philippe Rohrken, Bex Rimmington, and Geert Janssens—got their training plan, mentor, aero kit, and support from the best in their 2018 journey to Kona.[50] The four athletes had well-established spheres of influence and a credible sports history.

- Rachael Norfleet joined the team with over 16k Instagram followers.
- Bex brought decades worth of professional caliber racing in cycling and rowing. She raced professionally for Merlin and podium previous individual and tandem cycling events.
- Golo was the head coach of Rocket Racing and captain and coach of Tri Team Hamburg.
- Geert, having crashed in Kona and DNF the year before, seemed most prime for a comeback story.

Maybe it was disingenuous to sell the story of the underdog when Specialized plucked the best of the best age groupers in hopes that they would podium either overall or within their

---

50 "Introducing the 2018 Specialized Zwift Academy Tri Team!" YouTube (YouTube, April 24, 2018).

age groups at Ironman World Championships.[51] But to select the best age groupers seemed to be exactly the point; the problematic assumption was the label "age grouper" meant a story of an average Joe athlete who miraculously wins the biggest Ironman race of the year with the help of top-of-the-line equipment and one year of coaching.

By nature, these athletes needed to come in at a certain level. They needed to be primed to attain a podium spot at the largest triathlon event with the world's best athletes. This was built in as applicants needed to come in with at least a Zwift biking level of 12 and running level of 3 to be eligible to apply.[52] To give context, the baseline to reach level 12 takes about 30,000 experience points (XP), which is about 1,500 kilometers or 1,000 miles on Zwift.[53] It would be a stretch to think one year would be enough to elevate a triathlon hopeful to the level of the top five amateurs in the world; the selection was based on the best athletes in the world in their age group who would inspire and reach the sub-selected customer group that Zwift and Specialized hoped to reach.

To carve a value proposition in a sport with many incumbent tri teams (Zoot, Timex, Betty Designs), Specialized Zwift branded themselves as the most well-supported tri team. The individuals got thousand-dollar indoor kickers, full kits, a

---

51  "We Were Totally Wrong About Zwift Academy," Triathlete, December 22, 2018.
52  "2019 SPECIALIZED ZWIFT ACADEMY TRI TEAM TERMS & CONDITIONS," Zwift, accessed January 27, 2020.
53  Eric Schlange, "XP, Levels, and Unlocks in Zwift Ride," Zwift Insider, October 23, 2019.

sponsored training camp in Morgan Hill, California, and $1,500 for Kona qualification expenses.[54] The goal was to provide these age groupers with the best equipment and training for a world championship podium win.

So, what did Specialized and Zwift get in return? Brand amplification within the four teammates' spheres of influence. In the debut year, Specialized and Zwift needed to lean on the existing influence of the team members. Each member's individual account had better reach than the team's own social media channels.

The first couple episodes on the Specialized Zwift Academy YouTube channel garnered tens of thousands of views. This was modest engagement but isolated video traction, as there was no consistent following shown by the low number of views (a few hundred, at most 1k) on the individual vlogs through the six-month program length. It was through Rachael, Geert, Bex, and Golo's existing audience that the sponsors could deliver the marketing pitch. The athletes already did the work of building an audience.

The Specialized Zwift Academy Tri Team relied on the social media audience and athletes that these four team members reached. That seemed to be the strategy of engagement, as these were potential target consumers for the sponsors to engage with through the athletes' personal social media accounts and through the YouTube series. Geert Janssens

---

54 "Got What it Takes to Get on the Brand New Zwift Specialized Tri Team?" Triathlete, (Triathlete, February 23, 2018).

ended up not qualifying for Kona, finishing sixteenth in his age group[55] at Ironman Hamburg due to stomach issues.[56]

This left the other three athletes to race at Kona. Rachael Norfleet, unfortunately, didn't finish the World Championship race and ended up in the medical tent.[57] Bex Rimmington started strong on the swim, coming out of the water second in her age group, and finished the race in thirty-fourth place in her age group.[58] Golo finished twentieth in his age group, upping his forty-fifth place performance from the year before and cutting more than one hour off his time.[59]

In 2019, The Specialized Zwift Academy Tri Team expanded to offer eight athletes the chance to join the team. Wahoo, Science in Sport, and Roka put forth their sponsorship of the team.[60] Wahoo offered a full indoor training setup, or the pain cave with the KICKR, CLIMB, and HEADWIND, along with the Wahoo ELEMNT BOLT bike computers and TICKR X heart rate straps. Science in Sport came on as the team's fuel supplier and Roka provided the Maverick X wetsuits and Viper swimskins. There seemed to be more engagement

---

55  "2018 IRONMAN Hamburg," Ironman, accessed January 27, 2020.
56  "We Were Totally Wrong About Zwift Academy." Triathlete, December 22, 2018.
57  Rachael Norfleet, Instagram post, October 14, 2018.
58  Chris Harby, "Bex Rimmington Interview: Unfinished Business for Melton's Iron Lady," Melton Times, December 27, 2018.
59  "We Were Totally Wrong About Zwift Academy." Triathlete, December 22, 2018.
60  Gary, "Specialized Zwift Academy Tri Returns for 2019," endurancebusiness.com, December 21, 2018.

through the Zwift YouTube channel with a higher number of views. 2019 Zwift Academy Tri Team Camp in Morgan Hill had the most views of any video released, with just shy of 350k views.[61]

Learning from the previous year, Zwift Academy Tri Team selected eight athletes. Two of the eight had already qualified for Kona in 2018 and the other six had a good chance of qualification during 2019.[62] Craig Taylor, director of growth marketing for Tri and Run at Zwift, confirmed that the sponsors hoped for them to be great ambassadors, but also to have personalities.[63] But really it was their results that came through.

In 2019, four women on the team delivered what Zwift Academy Tri Team sought out to do during their inaugural year at the Ironman World Championships in Kona. Ruth Purbrook led with an overall female amateur win, and her teammate, Natia Van Heerden, finished third overall among female competitors. Maggie Walsh finished second in her age group and Yvonne Timewell third in her age group.[64]

Though the women clearly dominated, this did not diminish any of the contributions that the men made to the team. Phillip Herber finished fourth in his age group. Justin Lippert,

---

61   "The 2019 Specialized Zwift Academy Tri Team Training Camp," YouTube (YouTube, May 25, 2019).

62   Lars Finanger, "Kona Dreamin' with Zwift's Academy Tri Team," slowtwich.com, October 12, 2019.

63   Ibid.

64   Lars Finanger, "Kona Dreamin' with Zwift's Academy Tri Team," slowtwich.com, October 12, 2019.

who started Full Send Triathlon and 4x USAT National Champ within nine months between 2018 to 2019, captivated his social media audience throughout the year of representing both Full Send and Specialized Zwift Tri Team.[65]

Even though the contract stands at only one year, it seems like that is by design. Members of other tri teams build deep intra-team connections over years of being on the team, whereas Specialized Zwift Tri Team seems like a one-year acceleration, or incubator program. The one-year cliff allows Zwift and Specialized to reselect athletes that have the best shot at getting onto the podium (athletes can age-up, leave the sports, get injured, etc.) and cherry pick the stories that will be most successful.[66] The one-year sponsorship seems to be working, as amateur athletes get a platform to prove themselves and make connections in the industry. For example, Ruth Purbrook plans to take her sabbatical for work and go pro in 2020.[67] As long as Specialized and Zwift continue to provide one of the highest monetary sponsorships in the amateur triathlon world, it will continue to attract the strongest triathletes in the world.

Brands need brand ambassadors to promote their brand and grow positive feelings toward the brand because this contributes to top line growth. They can offer sponsorship and perks to incentivize brand promoters. Brands can also inherit a lot

---

65   Nick Hehemann, "Age Group Triathlete of the Year Justin Lippert Is Going 'Full Send' into 2019," Team USA, May 3, 2019.
66   Krabel Herbert, "On the throttle with Kona superstar Ruth Purbrook," slowtwich.com, October 21, 2019.
67   Ibid.

of benefits from individual athletes. Sponsor-ambassador partnership is a two-way street and both parties are crucial to the relationship.

## SEVEN

# SPONSOR-ATHLETE FIT

### FIT ENOUGH

For the brand-athlete relationship to work, it needs to be a fit on both ends. Brands will seek athletes that align with their brand vision and athletes should also screen for brands that match their own goals beyond the label of being a sponsored athlete. In a perfect world, any changes to athlete or brand goals would shift in the same direction, but that's not always the case. Athletes and brands can evaluate fit based on the type of sponsorship relationship first, but ultimately need to align on shared values for a long-term match.

Individual sponsorship contracts vary from company to company, but there are three broad tiers. The three tiers are pro contracts or individually negotiated contracts, brand ambassadors, and team sponsorships. Professional athletes usually negotiate contracts where they will get annual compensation and can then get bonuses based on race winnings or qualifications. I would lump the sponsored contracts of influencers/models/etc. into this category too. In recent times, there have been other structures of sponsorship outside of what pros negotiate. Brand ambassadors, really popularized by Lululemon, consist of grassroots influencers who promote a brand. Brand ambassador programs can vary a lot, but the framework has been proven successful, so there has been a rise in the popularity of brand ambassadors. Sponsorship can also come through a team or organization such as a bike shop team or the national team. Teams will usually have affiliated sponsors and company partnerships that trickle down to the team members.

## HEATHER FELL

Heather Fell has experienced all three types of sport sponsorship throughout her career: team sponsorship, individual brand sponsorship, and brand ambassadorship.

Going from a five-discipline sport to a three-discipline sport doesn't make the achievements come any easier. Heather Fell, a former Modern Pentathlon Olympic Silver Medalist, quickly transitioned to a triathlon career upon retiring from professional sports. Plymouth-born, sport was in her blood at a young age.[68] Her parents were amateur jump jockeys and Heather grew up on a farm in Devon located in southwest England.[69] [70] Heather trained with humble beginnings, from

---

68 "Heather Fell," Team GB, accessed January 27, 2020.

69 Sean Ingle, "London 2012: Heather Fell Fears Abrupt End to Her High-Five Dream," The Guardian (Guardian News and Media, March 24, 2012).

70 Graham Clutton, "London 2012 Olympics: Modern Pentathlon Star Heather Fell Cannot Face Prospect of Missing out on Final Shot at Gold," The Telegraph (Telegraph Media Group, April 5, 2012).

riding in the Pony Club to representing Brunel University to being on Team Great Britain.[71]

Sport was a big part of her life early on as she rode ponies, swam, and ran around as a toddler growing up on a farm.[72] As a child, she grew up swimming and horseback riding, before picking up shooting, and fencing. With the help of team members and community support from the Pony Club, an equestrian organization, as well as her school swimming coach, Heather was propelled into her Modern Pentathlon career. Heather became Junior World Champion when she was 20, which became the turning point of her sporting career. As a result, she saw professional sports as a viable career option and continued to train by swimming, fencing, and running for her university.[73] The rise in her career came at a perfect time, as Modern Pentathlon became more prominent on the international stage.

The Modern Pentathlon was added to the 2000 Olympics and a Pony Club teammate won the bronze medal at the games. Both of these events opened new opportunities for Heather in her sport and fueled her ambitions. She went on to podium multiple times at the World Champs in her early twenties. Between 2008 and 2012, Heather won golds and silvers at European and World Championships and World

---

71   "Heather Fell," Team GB, accessed January 27, 2020.
72   Sean Ingle, "London 2012: Heather Fell Fears Abrupt End to Her High-Five Dream," The Guardian (Guardian News and Media, March 24, 2012).
73   "Heather Fell," Global Triathlon Network, accessed January 28, 2020.

Cups, which gave her enough clout to be seriously considered for sponsorships.[74]

She recalls the pre-social media days where her first sponsorship came along from a highlight reel her coaches made along with some posters and brochures. After university, Heather came to a crossroad where she could pursue a career in physiotherapy as per her major or try going professional for Pentathlon. Her decision was made to train professionally after no jobs worked out.

She moved to Bath, United Kingdom and spent some time in the Great Britain National Training Center, but her tenure was truncated. Heather stated:

> *"I was used to being more in charge of my own training program and liked more independance I knew what worked for me. My coach back home knew me very well and we had a really strong relationship when I was a swimmer. Coming from a swimming background, you're quite mobile, swimmers have really mobile joints and that doesn't go well and running. Having studied physio, and being a swimmer I knew my body really well and the training involved just didn't suit me. I just kept getting injured and the doctors just said that I wasn't doing the prescribed rehab. Well, I was...it got very sour and with little warning, my funding was suddenly taken away from me. I was told to leave the training center a year later*

---

74 "Heather Fell Announces Retirement from Modern Pentathlon," BBC Sport, (BBC, January 9, 2014).

> *[after starting]... I had all my medical support taken, I got all my funding taken, and no job... I knew I had more and I wasn't ready to just leave it behind. So, I basically gave myself a year, if in a year's time, if I still wasn't going anywhere, then I was just going to say fair enough, I tried and I'll go and get a job."*

That marked the end of the first type of sponsorship Heather had through the UK Sport Lottery funding.

It was just the push Heather needed to move back to home a couple hours away from Bath and train exclusively with her own coach. Heather figured she would give herself one year before she threw in the towel. With something to prove though, she quickly secured her spot on the roster for the British Modern Pentathlon Senior Team within a year and qualified for the 2008 Beijing Olympics the following year. Heather Fell won the Silver Medal at the games vindicating all her efforts. She recalled:

> *"And then the rest is kind of history ... I won a [Olympic] medal, and everything changed again. There's suddenly so many more opportunities with sponsorship...In the UK, they do talent ID, but there's so much talent that isn't identified ...I obviously had some talent, but I'm sure other people had as much talent, but you don't get sponsorship until you've got the result and how do you get the result? And that's what say, tricky isn't it?"*

Parting with the national team ended up being the better career move for her. It also resolved some brand conflict of interest, as Heather had sponsorship with her own companies and the national team had relations with others. When Heather was affiliated with the national team, the modern pentathlon team was poorly managed with brand sponsorships coming and going. The benefits were kept within the organization for training or events. Athletes with a better track record like hers would have outside sponsorships to supplement whatever tiered funding they got from the governing body. If an athlete got too much funding from outside sponsors, the UK Sport capped government funding that a GB athlete received. Heather recalled that the CEO of the training center would say the athletes had to do a photo shoot for a specific brand, but Heather couldn't wear another clothing brand because she was sponsored by Adidas.

Adidas was her longest standing sponsor from 2007 to 2013. During this time, she also worked with an individual agent to help manage her partnerships. Before Heather qualified for the Olympic Games, Adidas gave her a free kit, which was a nice surprise because up until then she had to beg and borrow for her Pentathlon kits. Her swimming coach told her she needed to go to Adidas and figure out the exact payment of how much the company would pay her, if she won an Olympic medal.

All parties involved drafted up a contract with monetary compensation and clauses before the Games, but the contract wasn't actually signed before her podium. Adidas kept to the prospective agreement and paid Heather for the accomplishment. The company's gesture made Heather very loyal and she cultivated the longstanding relationships, which made her enjoy doing promo events and love working with the team.

A local haulage company gave Heather and her teammates free cars and gas as the owner wanted to support the athletes. Heather's most unexpected sponsor was a chicken company that consistently paid her, but she was frustrated with the lack of partnership. She also worked with French Connection at the time she found out she wasn't going to the 2012 London Olympics. Heather retired from Modern Pentathlon in 2014.[75]

In 2015, while getting business cards printed, her boyfriend met someone who knew the owners of BlueSeventy, a triathlon and competition swimwear company. They were based in Bath, UK and offered to give her a free wetsuit and entry to her first triathlon, which she didn't put too much thought into doing. BlueSeventy gave her everything she wanted from kits to wetsuits to goggles. There was no contract, no anything, just word of mouth and a long-standing relationship.

Around 2017, she got into longer distances via a cross-country ride where she was part of the Cannondale Girls cycle team. She was trying to solicit more sponsorships for the team and also got more press than the others, but still questioned whether she deserved the title with no former road cycling background. Heather did feel strongly about promoting women's sports and advocating, so she continued to pursue the opportunity. The experience made Heather seriously consider getting into triathlons.

---

75 "Heather Fell Announces Retirement from Modern Pentathlon," BBC Sport, (BBC, January 9, 2014).

For the first Ironman in 2017, Heather wanted to get some press for the companies that without a record supported her. She did much better than expected at the South Africa Ironman placing second in her age at her debut Ironman and got local TV exposure. This marked her brief time with a sponsorship through a team. Heather joined GTN, a YouTube channel, as a part of the Play Sports Network Media Company midway through 2017 and is still with them at the time of this writing. As a result, she has to forgo all of her individual sponsorships because the company has a whole sponsorship apparatus and structure.

Looking back, Heather preferred a brand ambassador role above others. She believed and still believes relationships need to be organic and genuine. Her most successful sponsorships were more partnerships. Under Team GB, Heather had no say and was on the receiving end of training and sponsorships that weren't aligned with her values or obligations to her individual sponsors. In contrast, Heather loved working with the Adidas team because they were fun and she wanted to go to the events and showings to support the brand that supported her through Modern Pentathlon. BlueSeventy was another great partnership. Heather wouldn't even self-proclaim that she was sponsored by BlueSeventy, but she was loyal to the brand because they wanted to help an amateur athlete. It was just a mutually beneficial relationship, as athletes get products and companies get press and social media coverage.

Heather iterated, the only way she would agree to partner was if she liked and would use the product. In contrast, Heather's sponsorship by the government was surface level. The organization wanted the numbers and bodies at the world stage. There were benefits such as health care, salary, and dedicated training centers, but the relationship wasn't deep. If athletes couldn't conform to the program, they were cut. In best sponsorship cases, there usually wasn't a salary compensation, only products and possibly being a part of the development process; however, there may be opportunities for speaking events or conferences where the companies could justify paying for a speaker.

Athletes can decide which type of sponsorship they feel more inclined to pursue. Maybe they are more inclined toward brand ambassadorships because they really love the brand products and want to join an ambassador program. Maybe they pursue the team sponsorship option because having a predetermined list of affiliate sponsorships is sufficient. Maybe, if their record or tout is big enough, they can negotiate individual contracts with brands.

## CAN'T BEAT BEALS

From the brand perspective, there can be a myriad of reasons why they offer a certain type of sponsorship. Wattie Ink, a triathlon clothing company, also has all three types of sponsorship. The company sponsors pros such as Cody Beals, Josh Amberger, Sarah Piampiano, and Rachel McBride. It also has an elite racing team, The Wattie Ink Elite Team, which has a rolodex of affiliate sponsors. Then, the company has a more conventional brand ambassador team, The Wattie Ink Hitsquad, where Wattie Ink acts as the primary clothing affiliation for these athletes. Evidently, for each of these tiers, Wattie Ink focuses on different considerations. Wattie Ink can cover a wider range of their brand strategy with each tier of sponsorship.

On May 7, 2019, Wattie Ink released a kit promo video starring Canadian triathlon professional Cody Beals. The video cuts through following Cody dressed in a suit and tie driving a yellow Lamborghini and vaporizing into a Tron-like universe speeding through a soundwave-like background in his purple, blue, and yellow kit.[76] This partnership came to fruition after years of holding off on a clothing sponsor.

Cody, who self-describes as a "nerd in jock's clothing" got his start in athletic competition in high school. He was abducted out of a high school math class to fill a fourth racing spot when the cross country team was in dire need of another person to race in the district championships. He then went on to race cross country, swim, and run track, which led him to the University of Queens in Ontario for running and academics. After suffering through an engineering-turned-physics degree, he decided to take a year off to pursue triathlon.

He did well enough that people around him encouraged him to pursue triathlon professionally and has really carved out a niche as transparently as possible as a professional triathlete with financial restraints, mental health issues, and the ups and downs of the sport.

Even though Cody quickly gained race success after his pro debut in 2014, he surprisingly stuck to stock equipment for longer than his industry peers. His attention to detail was

---

76  @wattieink, Instagram post, May 7, 2019.

a result of making a couple missteps earlier in his career. Cody mentioned:

> "So, I've had made a couple missteps with sponsorship over the years and learned some good lessons. And I've learned that it's really worth my time to carefully vet sponsors. So the process I go through now is pretty exhaustive, I set a cap of around eight to ten sponsors, unlike some athletes, who have like, you know, like a billboard on their race.... It looks like I've just learned from experience any more than eight to ten and I start to go a little bit crazy, and the quality of the services I'm offering really suffer. So, I'm only going to work with a handful of sponsors like that."

In 2016, Cody finally signed with Ventum, drawn to their technical details and also the break from traditional bicycle frame geometry.[77]

Cody took the same mindset to not compromising quality and wanting to build a relationship for his clothing sponsor. He said:

> "I really held out for years to find not only the right deal, in terms of, you know, the dollars and cents and [what] was on the table, but the right relationship with the people behind the company and the right product. You know, I'm not willing to compromise on something as fundamental as a bike, and equally

---

77  Cody Beals, "Ventum & My Quest for a Worthy Whip," Cody Beals, January 18, 2016.

> ... as fundamental as apparel. So, it was very similar. With a parallel to my bike sponsorship, I really held up for a long time [while] I talked to a lot of other companies, turned down offers.... I'm contented by my own equipment, without any strings attached [and] without any concessions on quality [until] I'm able to reach a level or make direct connections to work with a company that I really admire."[78]

It wasn't until 2019 that Cody signed with Wattie Ink, a triathlon clothing brand based in San Diego, after a breakthrough year for him winning five of the six races he started.

Cody was attracted to the top-notch quality and the "made in USA" ideology. What was even more important was he admired the marketing piece and snazzy eye-catching designs. He was looking to instill more spice and flavor into his look and brand as "nerd in jock's clothing" and Sean Watkins "Wattie" was able to help him reinvent his look.

He was pretty excited with Wattie and they both contacted each other simultaneously. The discussion went pretty fast and when Cody got to visit the factory in California, his impression was reinforced. He found no BS and genuine people on the staff. The Wattie Ink Elite Team and HitSquad also digitally welcomed him with open arms. He was excited to debut his vaporwave kit along with his Tron-like Ventum bike with teal-rimmed wheels.

---

78   Facebook (Wattie Ink, July 11, 2019).

Cody Beals was very selective with his sponsors and held out longer than the average well-performing professional. Evidently, the pros may have a much wider supply of sponsors to choose from; however, the same tact should be applied to amateur athletes looking for the right sponsor fit. A lot of times people want free stuff or like the idea of being sponsored by so-and-so brand. There should be careful consideration to whether a team and a set index of sponsors is the way to go, or if a brand ambassador program is better suited. Clarifying the exact fit may reduce bad blood down the road and also improve the sponsor-sponsored experience.

**PARTNERSHIPS**

In amateur sport sponsorship, there are alternatives to joining a sponsored team or local team. Individuals with more success may opt to partner directly with a brand. Brands may want to find the best athlete, or they may want someone who aligns with their business values. Within the elite triathletes, people switch teams to better suit their needs. Others may hold off a while before deciding which sponsors to represent. On the flip side, brands may change the direction of their sponsored team's requirements or change their focus year to year.

Looking at it another way, the sponsor-sponsored partnership is a business relationship. If there is still uncertainty as to which of the three types of sponsorship is more well-suited, perhaps take a step back and use conversation starter questions like:

- Are there alternatives to partnerships?
- Why this partner?
- Is this the best option?

These initial questions are from David Gage's book *The Partnership Contract*, which provides four questions to pry into whether the business partnership is a good fit.[79] The book isn't specifically intended for sport sponsorships, but the starting questions can be applied to these sponsorship structures. The so-called contract in the book is not legally binding but acts as a catalyst for important conversations. Both the athlete and brand sides should have ongoing conversations for honest collaboration and see if there are still shared values to increase the likelihood of a successful partnership.[80]

Shared values are crucial for a good fit in the athlete-brand relationship, but also important for partnership between affiliate brand sponsorships between brands and athlete. Wattie Ink and Quintana Roo, an American bike brand, found overlap in what they wanted for their ambassador program.

As mentioned in the previous chapter, American Bicycle Group CEO Peter Hurley and Sean "Wattie" Watkins found a natural partnership converging over the "made in USA" commonality.

---

79  Mark Rotella et. al, "THE PARTNERSHIP CHARTER: How to Start Out Right with Your New Business Partnership (or Fix the One You're In)," Publisher Weekly, June 28, 2004.

80  Paul J. Sauer, "How to Work with a Partner (Year After Year After Year)," Inc. Magazine, Oct 2004, 88-89

Tapping into Wattie Ink's amateur teams seemed like a proper fit for Quintana Roo. In doing so, Quintana Roo could inherit a light brand ambassador program without the set-up cost of starting its own. The alignment of Wattie Ink and QR's core values also helps start the partnership off on a good foot. As the partnership continues, it will hopefully elevate both companies' brand strategy.

**VALUABLE**
The sponsor-athlete fit is based on shared values and good partnerships. Parsing out those early on from both the brand and athlete side will set the foundation for the future.

# EIGHT
# REASSESSING THE RELATIONSHIP

---

## REEVALUATE, REPEAT

Once in the sponsorship relationship, athletes and brands both have the prerogative to reassess the relationship. It's not only an option, but absolutely necessary to get what they both need. Just as athletes set goals for times or finishes, they should also be clear as to whether they are heading toward their sponsorship goals. Athletes can break from a brand for multiple reasons. They may not be able to uphold the obligations from their end anymore or they may want or require a different type of relationship with a brand.

Team Wattie Ink's original gangster, Gerry Forman, decided not to reapply for the 2020 cycle at the age of eighty, after eight years on the team. Complications with his vision was making it difficult to get to race starts in the dark. He decided to not take an official team spot, but would still support the team in whatever capacity he could.

Brands also need to evaluate if they are getting the return on investment for sponsoring athletes. They can focus changes year to year for what they would like out of the athletes or in some cases, brands can stop sponsoring all together.

**TIMELINESS**

In 2018, Timex, a watch brand, ended its sponsorship of the "longest running triathlon team in the world."[81] The time capsule of the former website wrote:

> "In 2000, Team Sports, Inc., an established professional cycling team management firm, sat down with the marketing team at Timex Corp. The goal of this meeting: create a first-of-its-kind, world class, triathlon team, with the mission of supporting athletes who strive to push the limits of the mind and body. In 2001, the Timex Multisport Team was born. Over 17 years have gone by and the passion and strength of the Timex Team is greater than ever."

Between former Timex athletes selling their custom-painted Timex Trek bikes, social media posts thanking Timex for the patronage, and Slowtwich (triathlon) forums, it seemed that the team would be reorganized under another watch sponsor, Suunto; however, that was a mistaken perception.[82]

When Timex announced it would stop sponsoring the multisport team, it was a bittersweet parting. Trista Francis, an

---

81   Timex, accessed July 15, 2019

82   Trista Francis. Instagram post, December 28, 2018.

endurance athlete and coach, had been on the team since 2009, midway through the team's life span, and mentioned she was sad, but not surprised. It seemed like Timex wasn't accomplishing what they had hoped for during the last couple years. From the brand strategy perspective, it seemed that Timex was divesting from endurance sports at this stage in the corporate life cycle. At the same time, the length of the sponsorship and partnership was its lasting legacy.

Flash back to the team's inception almost twenty years prior. In 2000, Timex's marketing team hired Team Sports, Inc., a management team to create a one-of-a-kind world class triathlon team.[83] Each year thereafter, Timex recruited new athletes based on the marketing strategy for that year. Trista mentioned that one-year management focused on recruiting International Triathlon Union (ITU) and short course racers, whereas another year it wanted more Ironman World Championship qualifiers and coaches in the community.

The fabric of the team changed slightly from year to year, but the trend was that Timex athletes stayed on the team for years and years. Trista, like many of her former Timex teammates, never took their spots on the team for granted. The team received enormous support from partner affiliates like Trek Bicycles, Shimano, and Castelli to name a few.[84] With some of the best brand sponsors also came the pressure to represent Timex well. The Timex brand was so well known that Trista would be approached by strangers when she was racing and traveling throughout the years. Naturally,

---

83   Timex, accessed July 15, 2019.
84   Ibid.

over the years, athletes and corporate staff built deep relationships. The company genuinely thanked the athletes and gave each one of them an engraved Timex Signature Watch, when it was time for the athletes and the brand to go their separate ways.

When word got out that Timex was pulling out of sponsorships, other brands saw an opportunity to leverage the forty or so elite free agent athletes. The original Timex roster included forty-five athletes, including some of the best amateurs and professionals in the sport.[85] A handful of brands reached out to Team Sports, Inc., the management team that had been running the Timex Team for two decades, for a bid to cooperate. One brand won out.

On November 27, 2018, Suunto announced the inaugural year of its multisport team, seeking pro and amateur triathletes, along with ultrarunners, and other athletes, along with its ambassador team "Suunto Squad." The sponsored team "… will receive a fully-kitted athlete package from many industry leading partners, as well as media support and an annual team training camp. We are also outfitting the team with the new Suunto 9."[86]

From the public eye, it seemed like the Timex Team was organizing under the new watch brand Suunto; however, other than Suunto's hiring of Team Sports, that was the extent of the similarity to the former Timex Multisport Team. Team

---

85  Timex, Accessed July 15, 2019.
86  "CALLING TOP LEVEL ATHLETES: SUUNTO'S NEW MULTISPORT TEAM IS RECRUITING!," Suunto, November 27, 2018.

Suunto was not the old Timex team. Case in point, not all forty-five former Timex teammates transitioned over. Fewer athletes than expected joined the newly minted Suunto Multisport Team. Even more so, the brand strategy was completely different. Suunto's vision was a team of ultrarunners, triathletes, and off-road endurance athletes. The concept was a team of endurance athletes, not just triathletes.

Timex Team's legacy has its rightful place in the amateur sports sponsorship time line, but shifted resources off team sponsorship when the relationship wasn't what Timex needed anymore.

## TIME TO SAY GOODBYE

Timex's triathlon team involvement can be placed within the context of its long history to help understand why the brand divested from sponsorship.

Timex released its first triathlon watch in 1984. SVP of marketing, Mario Sabatini, at the time guided the marketing toward endurance sports cycling, running, and swimming.[87]

The following year, Sabitini took one thousand five hundred watches to the Hawaii Ironman.[88] Timex ended up spending $20 million in advertising for the cannon watch Timex Ironman during this time period. This would be one of the first licensed products for the Ironman brand. The race at

---

87 "THE ORIGINS OF THE TIMEX IRONMAN WATCH," cbw.com, August 28, 2019.

88 Ibid.

that time was relatively unknown, but in 1986, after Timex agreed to be an event sponsor, the event got on the map when an anonymous donor put up a $100,000 reward for first place.[89] [90]

With the success of the Timex Ironman and sports watches, Timex continued to innovate primarily sport watch technology, such as the watch face illumination of Indiglo, and the watch started to show up on the wrist of businessmen and doctors, branching out from the initial athlete target market.[91]

Through the '80s and '90s, Timex was the triathlete's watch. Going into the 2000s, Timex Multisport Team was a continuation of that marketing piece. By the new millennium, with other sport watch brands like Garmin, Suunto, and Polar having only one target market, Timex seemed to go back to the "personal and pop-culture nostalgia" feel with the core of affordable quality.[92] Other brands were now chasing cutting edge sport wearable technology, whereas Timex had had its time in previous decades.

---

89  "Timex, Walt Disney, Mickey Mantle & the Ironman Triathlon Watch," Ironman Triathlon Watch—A History of the Timex Company, accessed January 27, 2020.

90  Danielle Sarver Coombs and Bob Batchelor, American History through American Sports: From Colonial Lacrosse to Extreme Sports, vol. 3 (ABC-CLIO, 2012), 281.

91  "THE ORIGINS OF THE TIMEX IRONMAN WATCH," cbw.com, August 28, 2019.

92  Troy Patterson, "Why Timex Is the Best Watch for the Money," Bloomberg, March 9, 2019.

Because companies ultimately put up the dollars and cents to sponsor teams, the return on investment needs to be justified from a marketing stand point. As companies evolve and grow, some break into more arenas, sponsoring a wider array of athletes, while other companies divest.

**BEYOND THE RELATIONSHIP**

Pulling out of sponsorship isn't the only way that brands can choose to reassess their resourcing. Brands can also reevaluate what their goals of athlete sponsorship are to further the experience for both athlete and brand.

In 2019, Wattie Ink, marked its tenth year in the business. Sean "Wattie" Watkins, the founder of the company, had started it with $250 in his bank account and a pipe dream. Budding pro Heather Jackson, Wattie's then girlfriend and now wife, was the first pro athlete the new company sponsored, with no sign-on bonus or guarantee of success.[93] They both believed in a vision grounded in the collection of athletes and triathlon people before they printed their first apparel. A decade later, Wattie released a post describing the genesis of Wattie Ink, saying:

> "*Wattie Ink first existed in the minds of a few athletes who believed we could do something different in the triathlon market. Triathlon—if you weren't here yet or don't remember—needed a little kick in the butt ten years ago: a fresh look, a team approach to an*

---

93 "It's Who We Are—The Wattie Ink. Story," Wattie Ink, accessed January 27, 2020.

*individual sport, a community that wanted something bigger than personal achievements."*

Wattie's term "for athletes, by athletes" is the soundbite version of a brand centered around the people that make the brand, rather than the tangible goods. This is the original vision of the sponsored team and I can say it rings true from firsthand experience on the Wattie Ink Elite Team.

The Elite team covers continental North America, working with the USA and Canada. Each year, the application cycle sees over four thousand applications for a hundred or so available slots for this tier of sponsorship.[94] The counterpart team Wattie Ink Hitsquad is made up of more than five hundred athletes that love and represent the Wattie Ink clothing brand and are spread out all over the world. This team is a brand ambassador team with less stringent sponsorship requirements and obligations compared to the Elite Team. Members of the Hitsquad represent Wattie Ink and can have other sponsors of their own, whereas the Elite Team represent Wattie Ink along with a handful of affiliate brands.[95]

Tu Tran, team manager and director of team programs, managed the over one hundred Elite team members along with over five hundred Hitsquad members in 2019. Since joining the Elite team in 2014, Tu has brought his strong leadership background from being a marine and now working in tech to

---

94  Chris Bagg, "Wattie Ink. Turns Ten," Wattie Ink (blog), December 11, 2019.

95  Chris Bagg, "Join the W Family—Applications Open Today," Wattie Ink (blog), Sept 24, 2019.

managing a geographically dispersed team. For the team, Tu says his main job is being the liaison between the Wattie Ink factory and the sponsored teams being both the Elite Team and the Hitsquad. He also builds the affiliate partnership pipeline and deals with the sponsorship obligations from the individual members to the other partners and vice versa.

Not surprisingly, a lot of the longest-standing sponsors for both teams stemmed from personal relationships to triathlon pro Heather Jackson or Wattie himself: Herbalife24, a sport nutrition arm out of Herbalife, and Speedfil, a sports hydration company, just to name a few. Each member of the Wattie Ink Elite team has a relationship with the Wattie Ink brand, but each member also has a relationship with affiliate brands and Wattie Ink' partners. The triathlon community is small and inherited relationships are a big driving factor behind partnerships. At the same time, the majority of the other brands listed on the team kits are based on negotiations each year. Consistently reassessing what the affiliate brands are getting out of a partnership with the Wattie Ink teams allows both sides to commit to and invest in the relationship each year.

For the Wattie Ink teams, there is a mutually beneficial contract. To put it loosely, brands provide affiliate discounts on their products and contribute to the team budget, which funds team dinners, events, and so on, to grow the triathlon community and build camaraderie. In exchange, brands receive not only the move than five hundred potential customers already within the sponsored team, but also a grassroots marketing army.

Although once an affiliate brand comes onboard, they have access to the Elite and Hitsquad team, that doesn't automatically mean access to the Wattie Ink pros such as Josh Annenberg, Sarah Piampiano, Cody Beals, or even Heather Jackson, who are managed separately. In most cases, affiliate brands understand their part of the relationship with Wattie Ink. These partners see the value of sponsoring a team of elite amateur athletes. Pros don't usually sign with a collective of brands as they or their agents would manage each individual contract. As I've seen, for the pros, Wattie Ink is the pros' triathlon kit sponsor and pros have other sponsors for hydration, nutrition, and so on. The relationship is between the pros and Wattie Ink; affiliate sponsors to the Wattie Ink Teams are separate.

It's safe to say that there are a lot of relationships to be managed and looked at from year to year. Even for the Wattie Ink Elite Team, the network of the triathlon community is bigger than just the myriad of sports products or personal discounts and hasn't been a completely seamless journey. For how strategic the team set up is now, this was not always the case.

The previous team manager departed unexpectedly, and since Tu's tenure, the main tactic has been going back to the basics of investing in the relationships.

Upon the reevaluation of what the team should look like, the next evolution of the team is to move toward a more experiential exchange, rather than solely depending on contractual monetary or financial gains from the sponsorship contracts. The current market is super saturated, as many companies are doing the same thing. High-quality products and competitive prices isn't a competitive advantage anymore. How does a brand or team differentiate itself? How does it make an experience better? How can it build a community and make the human condition better?

In 2019, Wattie Ink held a VIP rooftop afterparty following Oceanside 70.3, an iconic half Ironman usually graced by the presence of the top triathlon pros each year. The event was centered around fundraising for Fxck Cancer, an organization raising funds and awareness for cancer research. During Wattie Ink Elite Team Camp, a weeklong training camp filled with swimming, biking, and running, affiliate sponsors came for info talks and giveaways. This added more context to the brands that support our teams. The events sponsored by the Wattie Ink Team sponsors enrich the triathlon experience beyond the monetary end goal or materialistic component. The whole ecosystem helps teammates and others socialize, continue to build connections, and ultimately, brand loyalty. As Tu states:

> "The brand and culture are the same and the more you can amplify through partnership the more there is a natural synergy and moving from 'I love this product' to 'I love the brand.'"

The next phase of a successful partnership is one that creates a virtuous cycle for the larger community. To achieve this, existing sport sponsorship relationships need to be good to provide a solid foundation. Brands reassessing their partnerships and brands understanding their roles in providing athlete sponsorship contributes to the overall goal. The collaborations can grow the community and create mutually beneficial partnerships. On the flip side, without clarifying the purpose of athlete sponsorship or partnership between two brands, one party can feel they are not getting their return on investment. It can also dampen future relationship and collaboration opportunities that could grow the sports community.

The relationships built are dynamic. For all parties involved, they should reassess what they are getting out of the partnerships. It should be beneficial and collaborative. If the relationship deviates, there is room for course correction; however, partnerships can dissolve amicably if individual actors know what their goal is and stay true to their true north. Ultimately, brands need to manage their corporate marketing direction and athletes may have their own reason to stay or leave a relationship.

**NINE**

# CONTENT IS KING

———

In today's digital age, content is king. Brands need content for marketing. A bigger and bigger impetus to push brand content through channels such as social media, websites, video streaming, and so on is becoming the norm. Sponsored athletes play a crucial role in a brand's content strategy. Let's take a look at the brand that gave content wings.

**GIVES YOU WINGS**

Red Bull pioneered sponsoring nonmainstream sports. Currently, over 750 athletes are flying the Rebel flag around the world.[96]

Since 1987, Dietrich Mateschitz, co-founder of Red Bull, has been creating his own market for his energy drinks.[97] The brand's marketing strategy has flown in the face of traditional marketing, but really begs to be reckoned with, as it has not relied on the product or traditional advertising to

---

96 "Athletes," Red Bull, accessed January 27, 2020.
97 "Company," Red Bull, accessed December 20, 2020.

gain loyal fans. Red Bull didn't launch as a highly coveted product nor did it easily get distribution rights to sell in any of the markets it started out in. Instead, Red Bull created a niche for itself in the form of extreme marketing, or content creation, to generate a fervent fan base.

After a trip to Thailand and learning that one of the top ten taxpayers in Japan made his wealth selling energy drinks, Mateschitz decided to create an energy drink based off of water, sugar, caffeine, and taurine. Back in Europe, he asked an old school friend, Johannes Kastner, to design a commercial can and logo. After going back and forth, with Mateschitz rejecting all of the samples Kastner provided, Kastner submitted one last proposal "Red Bull—gives you wings." This has been the iconic Red Bull slogan to this day.

Red Bull, recognized by people all over the world and synonymous with its jaw-dropping content, had a rough start. After launching in Austria, Red Bull suffered millions of dollars of loss making Mateschitz realize the market was too small to sustain the business. In the '90s, he looked toward tapping into Hungary, Germany, and the rest of the European markets.

With an unprecedented $12 million deficit in England alone, Mateschitz fired the whole team and resorted to grassroots marketing to save on traditional advertising. He targeted students that had influence in their social circles to create buzz. He also recruited a group of college students to drive around in small cars with a big Red Bull can strapped on top and offer samples at parties. By the turn of the century, Red Bull's sales in England hit two hundred million cans, completely turning around the business. Using these lessons in England, in April 1997, Mateschitz broke into the US market. In the states, swarms of Volkswagen Beetles with huge Red Bull cans strapped to their backs began to show up at local watering holes.[98]

From this grassroots marketing, Mateschitz conjured up another idea: breaking into extreme sports. Since then, the brand has monetized its content machine unlike any other brand. As Lieb states, "Red Bull has aligned its brand unequivocally and consistently with extreme sports and action."[99] The content was so core to Red Bull's identity that in 2007, Red Bull created Red Bull Media House as the umbrella for Red Bull's massive print, television, online, and feature film production.[100] The studio was created to distribute content through other partner channels. Some of the content that Red Bull Media House has produced includes *Space Dive*, a documentary of the base jump from space, and *Red Bulletin*, Red Bull's magazine. As Nick Amies, a freelancer for Red Bull Europe wrote, "… The promotion of the brand comes through the activities…"[101] Red Bull's content activity is promoting its brand.

The brand has become inextricably associated with the stunts it pulls. The Red Bull Stratos mission is the best story of

---

98  Gerhard Gschwandtner, "The Powerful Sales Strategy behind Red Bull," Selling Power, March 1, 2012.
99  James O'Brien, "How Red Bull Takes Content Marketing to the Extreme," Mashable, December 19, 2012.
100 Ibid.
101 Ibid.

the content machine's reach. On October 14, 2012, Red Bull released a one-and-a-half minute video garnering over 45 million views on YouTube.[102] The quest was to prove that "humans could survive accelerating through the sound barrier in free fall and land back on earth safely."[103] The mission that shattered five world records entailed a 128,000-foot free fall above Earth, which was completed by Austrian parachutist and base jumper Felix Baumgartner. He is best known for completing an unprecedented freefall flight across the English Channel using a carbon wing and base jumping off Rio de Janeiro's Christ, the Petronas Towers in Kuala Lumpur, and Taipei 101 tower.[104]

Eight million people tuned in to watch the feat at the same time.[105] The five years of preparation, multiple test runs, and work that a team of scientists put in culminated into four hours and twenty-two minutes of free fall and nine hours and nine minutes of descent.[106]

Custom technology and years of research cost the company around $65 million, based on a speculative calculation.[107]

---

102 "Felix Baumgartner's supersonic freefall from 128k'—Mission Highlights," YouTube (YouTube, October 14, 2012).
103 "Red Bull Stratos," Red Bull Stratos (blog), accessed January 27, 2020.
104 Ibid.
105 Ashling O'Connor. "Felix Baumgartner's plunge from stratosphere breaks broadcast records." The Australian, October 16, 2012.
106 "Red Bull Stratos," Red Bull Stratos (blog), accessed January 27, 2020.
107 "Red Bull Invests $65M on Space Jump as More Than 8 Million Watch on YouTube," Sport Business Daily, October 16, 2012.

This was an extremely high marketing spend for arguably fifteen minutes of fame, but what Red Bull achieved was a digital marketing feat that shook the world. Over twenty videos in the Red Bull Stratos Series are on YouTube, many with millions of views.[108] The Red Bull Stratos website provided a landing page for the interviews, blogs, and interactive pages for the event. On the one-year anniversary, Red Bull Media House, along with BBC and National Geographic, released the documentary *Space Dive*.[109]

The feat that captured the human imagination and limitless sentiment spilled over to Red Bull sales. According to research firm IRI, Red Bull sales rose 7 percent to $1.6 billion in the US, six months after the jump.[110]

The return on investment may not have been there in terms of surface-level financial, but Red Bull seemed to gain brand recognition that can't be captured in dollars and cents. Red Bull has consistently allocated a sizable portion of its revenue to marketing. In 2004, Red Bull spent $600 million, or 30 percent, on marketing and a decade later its marketing budget is still high at roughly $2.2 billion on marketing, of its $6.7 billion in revenue in 2012. Of the marketing expenditure,

---

108 "Red Bull Stratos—World Record Freefall," YouTube, YouTube, October 15, 2012.
109 "Red Bull Stratos," Red Bull Stratos (blog), accessed January 27, 2020.
110 Natalie Zmuda, "Red Bull's Stratos 'Space Jump' Wowed the World—While Selling a Lot of Products," Ad Age, September 2, 2013.

about 20 percent, or $440 million, is spent on sports events and athletes.[111]

This tactic to create buzzworthy content contributes to Red Bull's brand, which is why the company keeps investing in these spectacles.

Red Bull continues to break into new places and follow the arch of their previous success, understanding that the content around their sponsored athletes is just as crucial to their brand. Red Bull invested heavily in eSport in 2008.[112] It mirrors the company's initial effort, going after extreme sports as a gateway toward more mainstream sports. It took on the market, capturing a complete monopoly for sports that all other sponsors had overlooked. In doing so, the legion of extreme sport athletes content continues to garner exposure for Red Bull. Along with Red Bull Media House, the company is able to monetize on all the content created around the legion of worldwide athletes. The athletes receive financial support and Red Bull "wings" to fly toward their goals and, in turn, Red Bull receive content that the masses buzz about for years to come.

---

[111] Wieners, Brad. "Q: When Is a Cliff Dive Good for Sales? A: When It's Sponsored by Red Bull." Bloomberg, May 25, 2013.

[112] "Getting 'It': What Brands Can Learn from Red Bull about Marketing in ESports," Digital Surgeons, April 17, 2018.

## CONTENT REVOLUTION

Red Bull may be one of the early adopters to this content marketing strategy, but in recent times it's become more and more prevalent.

In a 2014 Harvard Business Review, the Content Marketing Revolution mentioned that nine out of ten companies now use content marketing. The preference is that 70% of customers would rather hear about a brand through content than an ad.[113] He argues, "When it's done right, brand publishing encourages companies to mine internal resources and expertise in order to become intellectual agents."[114] Brands need to distribute information relevant to their audiences. Their athletes, employees, founders, and so on, are all part of their human capital arsenal, which brands can tap into for stories. The content can, therefore, be used to disseminate relevant information to grab the attention of target consumers and build brand loyalty. Sponsorship is definitely one way to facilitate that relationship.

Red Bull is the most notable early mover on content marketing branding, but many other sports brands such as Nike, Adidas, Salomon, Jaybird, etc., also engage in high levels of content marketing. Brands like Rapha, a luxury cycling clothing brand, create content integral to its branding. Rapha has a YouTube Channel called Rapha Films that produces content relevant to Rapha's target consumer.

---

113 "What Is Content Marketing?," Content Marketing Institution, accessed January 27, 2020.

114 Alexander Jutkowitz, "The Content Marketing Revolution," Harvard Business Review, July 1, 2013.

In 2009, the Rapha Continental was born. Stemming from the desire to get back to the "lost art of cycling," Daniel Wakefield Pasley (DWP) peaked Rapha's interest enough to buy in. The partnership sparked a beautiful series named the Rapha Continental. DWP was then riding a lot and also building his writing and art career, but he was fascinated by the backroads and longer self-supported journeys—a ride that instilled the spirit of adventure and exploration. The objective wasn't touring or racing, but that didn't take away from how substantial the rides were. They were "epic rides" as the Rapha marketing team would coin but would soon outgrow the terminology. It was a collaboration engendering beautifully composed videos and articles spanning across continents and events.

The group was just under twenty in total and included amateur riders Joe Staples, James Seiman, Samuel Richardson, Tony Pereira, Aaron Erbeck, Ryan Thomson, Greg Johnson, Ira Ryan, Cole Maness, Jeremy Dunn, Pierre Vanden Borre, Pete Rbijono, Dan Lagiois, Pers North, and Richard Bravo—none of whom were the young professional riders chasing podium finishes and crushing tours. Most had some years under their belt and some age in the loose bracket of their late thirties. All were definitely fit and in shape. They had their professional vocation that wasn't just cycling and were far from the days of boyhood innocence and naivete. About half the riders were on the East Coast and the other half were on the West Coast. They would hop into vans and ride beautiful, under-explored routes. They had support crews and a team to capture the special moments. They themselves were great storytellers with help from their collective videography, photography, writing, and photojournalism backgrounds. As

I scroll through each of their bios and all eighteen segments of the project, I can't help but be drawn into the arch.

Through the Rapha Continental series, the company gained traction without the model of traditional marketing. It has also shaped much of the core identity and the marketing of the brand today. Rapha strives to evoke emotion. It wants the audience to be excited about what they are doing and identify with the aspirational rider. It homes into the lifestyle brand.

Brands being successful in content marketing have great storytellers and content. The members of the group selected for Rapha Continental were all superb storytellers. Rapha has expanded into more arenas, rather than epic roads and epic rides. It now has series featuring the Education First (EF) professional cycling team going out and racing non-tour rides. Rapha creates and maintains a library for fans to engage with and inevitably increase exposure to the brand and its products.

**THE BOULDER PROBLEM**
Moving away from strong brands and established presence. Content has become integral to how individually sponsored athletes create credibility. Professional rock climbers rely on their social media presence and brand sponsorships to make a living. Unlike other lifestyle sports like snowboarding or cycling, rock climbing doesn't center around established competition like sporting events or races, which provide an inherent structure to extract content and stories. Not too much monetary incentive is involved and government support varies across nations. Producing captivating stories and

disseminating media is the industry norm for professional rock climbers. Historically, magazines acted as a gatekeeper to which athletes would gain exposure, but with the digital age, content is much more democratized. Brands bank on sponsored professional rock climbers to convey the adventure and feelings of awe, which brands can commercialize and sell to target customers.[115]

Alex Honnold, the most accomplished climber in the world, chose Elizabeth Chai Vasarhelyi and Jimmy Chin to film his attempt to free solo El Capitan in Yosemite. Vasarhelyi and Chin originally approached Honnold to craft a film about his climbing accomplishments in general, but Honnold verbalized that if they wanted to shoot, the only film he wanted to make was his attempt at soloing El Capitan. Vasarhelyi and Chin didn't initially agree. In fact, they took months to contemplate. The technicality and perfection required to summit the 4,000 feet of vertical gain meant any misstep could be Honnold's last.[116] In the end, Chin and Vasarhelyi decided to take on Honnold's proposal after Chin had a talk with another established climber named Jon Krakauer. Krakauer rationalized that Honnold was going to climb El Capitan regardless if there was a film crew. If this was a very worthy endeavor to capture on film and share with the world, then Vasarhelyi and Chin's team were the best crew to do so.

---

115   Guillaume Dumont. "The Beautiful and the Damned." Journal of Sport and Social Issues 41, no. 2 (April 2017): 99, 106-108.

116   Jason Guerrasio, "'The Directors of Oscar-Winning Documentary 'Free Solo' Explain Why They Made the Risky Decision to Film Alex Honnold's 3,000 Foot Climb up El Capitan without a Rope," Business Insider, February 24, 2019.

Vasarhelyi and Chin, along with their assembled team of filmmakers and professional climbers, put immense detail into shooting what became the National Geographic film *Free Solo*. With her talent for understanding the core narrative prior to collecting footage, Vasarhelyi committed to getting the "honest moment." This was different than industry precedent that was usually transactional with a brand to just get the shot.[117] The care to the piece created a documentary that won an Oscar and added another wild feat to Honnold's achievements.

The film benefitted Honnold's sponsors, which include brands like North Face; the brand updated his bio and released climbing products for Honnold's fans to purchase. Other sponsors like Black Diamond, La Sportiva, and Maxim Climbing Ropes were discretely featured in the film. The documentary also had positive spillover to Alex Honnold's own foundation (Honnold Foundation), which supports solar initiatives to reduce environmental impact.[118] The caliber of content not only captured an athletic achievement and emotion in a time capsule, but also allowed audiences all over the world to engage with the story. The story resonated extremely well, and when Honnold and the crew toured all over the world to promote the film, he was suddenly launched into unprecedented stardom.

*Free Solo* is a prime example of the quality of content a top athlete can produce and the spillover benefits brands and

---

117 Lisa Chase, "Free Solo's Director Doesn't Give a F**k About Climbing," Outside Online, September 12, 2018.
118 Honnold Foundation, accessed January 27, 2020.

sponsors get. Producing and diffusing content is now a part of an athlete's job and there has been a shift for companies to expect athletes to provide media content. It's embedded in the athlete proposition. It is crucial to how athletes gain fans, represent their sponsors, and build reputation.

**TALBOT COX MEDIA**

The explosive growth of Talbot Cox's videos has proven how paramount great content is in today's sponsorship age. Talbot has always been fascinated by the behind-the-scenes, but also saw a market opportunity. Professional athletes wanted to share their stories, but someone needed to step in to help them with content and alleviate the time demands for production. Talbot provided his service and fans have been eager for this type of athlete content since. In 2019, Talbot crossed over one million views for his Kona series, a collection of YouTube videos giving behind-the-scenes looks at top professional triathletes.

Talbot was obsessed with cycling and triathlon at a young age, enough to be interested in the behind-the-scenes look at Lance Armstrong, aided by the photographs from renowned photographer Elizabeth Kreutz. Talbot started racing triathlons at the age of nine, eventually jumpstarted his own kids' triathlon team, registered the @ironmantri Instagram handle, which Ironman eventually approached him to buy for $500. To say he was into triathlon would be an understatement as Talbot divulged his dream was to race and win Kona.

Talbot grew up in Oklahoma City in a family with ten kids, five girls and five boys. With a full house, Talbot was socialized at a young age to read people really well and understand when he crossed a line. It later helped him become a really strong relationship builder and, along with his hard-working entrepreneurial spirit, to be the number one name disrupting the triathlon content world. His path wasn't super linear, but his hustle and passion landed him on top.

After dropping out of university, Talbot moved to Boulder, Colorado to join a software bootcamp. He knew traditional schooling wasn't for him and had other brothers who were pretty successful as software engineers, so he followed in their footsteps.

In 2016, Talbot picked up a camera and started shooting his then-girlfriend Ellie Salthouse, a triathlon pro. Being in Boulder, a popular training ground for triathlon and cycling, he found himself in the epicenter of the sport. He was then working a full-time job in tech, but didn't love it, so he started to shoot triathlon races. He challenged himself and gave himself the benchmark that if he could make half his income as a photographer, it would give him enough reason quit his tech job. At the same time, his full-time job started to suffer as he was pursuing his passion for content creation. He was eventually forced to quit his desk job, as his boss saw he wasn't producing quality work anymore. Talbot dabbled in vlogging, social media, and started to pick up paid freelance work for triathlon organizing bodies like Super League and Island House.[119]

---

119 "I QUIT MY JOB! || Vlog 1," YouTube, (YouTube, August 31, 2017).

Talbot's original plan was to be a YouTube vlogger, stating he couldn't build the clout as fast as he wanted to:

> *"And so I'm sitting right here. And I'm like, 'I can do this because I started doing daily vlogs.' And then I slowly noticed, no one was watching. And I'm like, how can I make money, shoot athletes, and create content that people love to see and build my own brand? ... And [when] I finally figured out, I'm like, perfect. [I'll] have the athletes just do their normal training day. And I will go and I will record them and make a vlog of them, like a blog. And then I will sit down at the end of the day, interview them, and ask them about their day. And then I'll put it all together with cool dubstep music that people love and get them amped up. And that's what I'll do."*

He leveraged the credibility of professional athletes with their existing fan base and his passion for peeling back the curtains, inspired by his childhood love for the behind-the-scenes looks of Lance Armstrong in the Tour de France, Josh Cox's 2009 videos, Ryan Hall training for the Boston Marathon, and Specialized Bicycle's "48 hours with Tim Don" to provide behind-the-scenes footage of world-class athletes.[120][121]

In line with Talbot's triathlon forte, he pitched Gwen Jorgensen, Olympic triathlon gold medalist at Rio in 2016, and

---

120 "Olé | The Ryan Hall Boston Marathon Workout," YouTube, (YouTube, April 22, 2009).

121 "48 Hours of Training with Tim Don," YouTube, (YouTube, May 31, 2011).

her husband Patrick Lemieux with the idea for a YouTube channel, seeing there was an opportunity to grow her social media presence. Before Pat got back to Talbot with a confirmation, Gwen Jorgensen announced her retirement from triathlon in November of 2017.[122] In an interview with Marni on the Move, Talbot recalled:

> "And then like a few days later, they announced that she's quitting triathlon. I'm like, 'Wait a second. What are you talking about? And we were supposed to be going to Tokyo in four years' time for triathlon.' I never knew about this running thing. So, I mean, that was simply like the first running race I ever shot in my entire life going out to shoot Gwen at the Husky Classic. Just before that, I mean, I think my sister did like an indoor track meet the week before and ... they're running around with my camera just trying to figure [it] out, because it's so different 'cause I'm so used to just shooting triathlon."

At the same time, Talbot had an inkling that there was proof of concept within the triathlon world too. In October of 2017, he started out with the "24 hours with" series with whichever triathlon pros would give him the time.[123] His first athlete was Jeannie Seymore, and then he filmed with American pro Tim O'Donnell. Armed with a framework and concept, he reached out to Canadian pro Lionel Sanders. Talbot knew Lionel's main sponsor was Garneau, a bike brand, so he pitched that he could get twenty thousand views per video

---

122 "Talbot Cox," Marni on the Move (podcast), August 11, 2018.
123 "Talbot Cox" YouTube, accessed January 27, 2020.

for a total of three videos. That would be exposure to sixty thousand views. Right before Kona, Talbot tested it with one more Australian pro, Luke McKenzie, before he completed two videos of Lionel. After he released the videos, the views exploded to over ninety thousand views.[124] Talbot realized this was his proof of concept and that he needed to keep going.

Talbot's competitive advantage was how closely he followed the triathlon scene. Talbot made a risky bet that paid off immensely.

> *"So, I just jump on Instagram, and I messaged this girl who I thought was gonna do really good because I love following the sport. And I'm like, 'Lucy Charles is going to do incredible this year.' And I messaged Lucy. ... an underdog, and no one knows who she is. So, I made this video for her.... I'm like, 'Just get ready. This is a top contender for the race. She'll be first out of the water,' and people are like, 'Oh piss off, you,' and 'She's not gonna ... be first on the water, blah, blah. She's gonna get smoked.' And I'm like, 'Oh, no, she is.' And then I made this video of her. And then I just started pumping these videos. And then Patrick Lange messaged me on Instagram because I posted a poll and I was like, 'Who should I do a video for next?' And then ... my Instagram [was] just exploding. I had two thousand seven hundred followers. When*

---

124 "Talbot Cox," Marni on the Move (podcast), August 11, 2018.

> *I hit Kona last year, I think I left [with] like fifteen thousand."*[125]

In May of 2018, he reached ten thousand YouTube subscribers just after one year of quitting his job as a software developer.

Talbot also homed into the timing of his work, recognizing his competitive advantage:

> *"But yeah, I think the main thing that I tried to do is get the images and get them to the athletes as quick as I can. Speed is the name of the game and that's what I have learned. And the second I get [done] shooting a race, I'm straight to my computer [and] click the "edit all my profiles" presets. And I'm pushing my downloads to all the athletes. I'm like, 'Emma Coburn, here you go.' It's like tweeting … Emma Coburn. 'Hey, here your pictures, Gwen Jorgensen.' I'm like, 'Hey, can [you] get these to Shalane, Colleen Quigley, like all those runners?' But not only that, like [it's] the same thing for triathlons. I've became real good friends with them, and now they all know that I have the images. And so they'll come to me, my galleries, my website. That's where they can get images. They know they're going to be available within an hour of the race, versus waiting on the other photographers that might take a few days and things like that."*

---

125   Ibid.

He continues to create content and produce triathlon and running videos to grow the community and get people excited about these pros.

He relies mainly on his YouTube channel and professional athlete hires (Gwen Jorgensen and Mirinda Carfrae), which earn him monetary compensation that's about $3,500, according to an Instagram story on July 11-12, 2018. Based on the approximation in 2018, Talbot actually makes a modest amount by today's standard, but this income is still core to how he gave up a desk job to chase his passion. He is extremely entrepreneurial, always finding ways to monetize. From his modest beginnings hanging Christmas lights in Oklahoma during the winter triathlon off-season, he now creates merchandise and travels the world to shoot his most respected athletes.

He concludes:

> "I call myself not, like, a photographer, and not a videographer, just basically, like you mentioned, a content creator that could go with these athletes like Lionel Sanders, Gwen Jorgensen, Tim and Rinny.... and it's basically [creating] content where it is. It's an ease for them that they don't have to think about getting an image, they don't have to think about getting the content. But not only that, it's on a professional level. So, whether I post a picture or they post a picture, it's done professionally. And the level of professionalism that goes into it, which ultimately, we hope helps the sport in the long run and pushes other athletes to be more professional ... not only that, but it pushes

*brands to want to sponsor these athletes in the long run, because they have a big social media following."*

What Talbot has identified is something the sport of triathlon really lacked, which was behind-the-scenes and real-time footage. There was a dearth of quality content when he started. Managing websites like TimandRinny.com or GwenJorgensenmedia.com for a couple of his clients, he has been trying to take it to the next level and has provided a content pool for their sponsors.

Now, he manages the assets weekly and puts more photos and more content in them, so if any of their sponsors need photos, they have everything with one download. The content ultimately gives the athletes more credibility and engagement and brings fans along on the journey, which grows the fan base for the sport.

Content is now more relevant than ever. Brand ambassadors act as agents for content and brands use content to create positive sentiments about the brand. Fans and audiences can engage with the brand and athletes through content, and brands sponsor athletes for this type of cooperation. Professional athletes may have more resources to produce high-quality content, but amateur athletes have the opportunity to still provide value to other sponsored brands through the multiple channels that brands are now expected to engage with.

# TEN
# FUTURE IS FEMALE

---

## FEMALE TIDE

What's next for the brand-athlete paradigm? Whether people are ready for it or not, rising influence of increased female participation in sports, women's purchasing power, and highly vocal advocates will shift old paradigms of sponsorship. All of these factors and more, whether proactive or reactive, will shift brands to see the value of female athletic sponsorship.

## OLD PARADIGM

Before I delve into the future, it helps to ground us in the past. Let's take women's skiing, for example.

Female skiers like Sarah Burke carved out a space for women in skiing. Equal representation was never the default. Burke was a freestyle skier (a type of skier who specializes in skiing and aerial tricks) who was one of the first to bring skis into the half-pipe. She was one of the few women in the space and the first to land a 1080 (three full revolutions) in competition.[126] In 2012, an accident on a half-pipe training run that severed her vertebral artery, cutting off blood to her brain, devastated the skiing community. In her wake, Burke left a legacy by ushering women into a sport dominated by men. She fought for her place to compete with the boys when competitions didn't explicitly bar her from entering. Because of her, the X Games began including women's freeskiing half-pipe and slope style events, making it an early sport offering equal prize money for both genders.[127]

For Sophia Schwartz, a former US Team mogul skier, mentioned Sarah Burke to give context to the male-dominated skiing environment. She remembers one interaction in particular that showed just how difficult gender equality was. Sophia had her first sponsor interaction as a preteen. She remembers getting free ski poles and goggles in middle school. Her coach recommended she meet with Smith, a snow optics brand, at thirteen. The interaction with the company rep was awful. Sophia remembers the rep pulling out a contract to make a point. First, Sophia was female, second, she was in the nonmainstream sport of moguls, and third, she had no potential. She felt slapped in the face, and thankfully Scott, another winter accessory brand, ended up comping her gear. Later on, she switched over to POC Sports, then Giro and amalgamated sponsors like Honey Stinger, Zipline Ski, Flylow Gear, and Fischer Sports.

---

126 Amy Donaldson, "Sarah Burke Succumbs to Ski Injuries," Deseret News, January 19, 2012.

127 Rachel Axon," Sarah Burke left lasting legacy on Olympics before death," USA Today, February 18, 2014.

Even when systemic barriers (overt inequality) were removed, it still took a lot of time for the culture to catch up. When female athletes did get to compete and were given the same respect as male athletes, women still had to prove their right to be there. Not only in skiing, but also in early cycling, male sports were the norm and female sports were the sideshow.

So, what can we do about it?

**GIRLS KICK BALLS**

Dr. Daniel Kelly, the faculty director and a professor at Georgetown's MPS Sports Industry Management Program, has seen how underrepresented actors (coaches and athletes) navigate the sports world. Through his work, the consistent themes he sees are:

1. Underrepresented people will usually get one chance.
2. These opportunities have scarce resources.

To combat these obstacles and level the playing field, Dr. Kelly recommends finding actors that will provide financial support (sponsorship having its place) and giving underrepresented groups a voice. His focus has been on African American athletes and coaches; however, there are relevant takeaways that can apply to women in sports.

Women do not have as much financial backing as their male counterparts. From 2011 to 2013, female sponsorship accounted for 0.4 percent of the $106.8 billion spent during the three-year time frame.[128] That is a minuscule fraction of the category that makes up the majority of sponsorship spending.

Sport sponsorship spending makes up about 70 percent of total sponsorship spending.[129] In 2018, allocate sponsorship money is growing at 4.9 percent year to year, which amounts to about $65.8 billion of predicted spending.[130] Companies are budgeting and putting resources into sport sponsorship; it is just not making it into the hands of a diverse group of athletes.

Brands, therefore, have an opportunity to allocate sponsorship to women. Assos, a swiss cycling clothing company, targeted female athletes like Kym Nonstop and Rebecca Rusch to break into the US market. Under Armour's SVP, Adrienne Lofton, has spearheaded how UA approaches the female consumer. They approached women as a gender, not a category.[131]

Even more than using a sponsored athlete as a conduit, though it is much needed, larger organizations can put dollars behind equality. It takes reputable organizations and existing orders and stakeholder buy-in to foster the female space. In 2017, FC Barcelona, arguably the most famous

---

128 Charlotte Rogers, "Why brands must rethink their approach to women's sports sponsorship," MarketingWeek, February 8, 2018.

129 "Sponsorship Spending Report," IEG, 2015.

130 "Sponsorship Spending Trends, 2014-2018 (Predicted)," Marketing Charts, accessed January 27, 2020.

131 "Adrienne Lofton, Under Armour," Sports Business Journal, September 11, 2017.

soccer clubs internationally, pledged to sponsor a National Women's Soccer League (NWSL).[132] Though starting a NWSL franchise may cost less than the alleged $200 million needed to start a Major League soccer franchise, money and organization cannot be overlooked.[133] FC Barcelona providing financial backing and signaling support is crucial, as the NWSL is the third iteration of the United States' attempt at establishing a national women's soccer federation. Its predecessors Women's Professional Soccer and the Women's United Soccer Association never made it past the third season. However, guaranteed success is still hard fought. Two teams in Kansas City and Boston folded, leaving nine NWSL teams.[134] But, savvy business decisions can propel a women's soccer franchise to prosper and create more opportunities for success.

Perhaps, female soccer can finally reap the benefits of what it's always deserved. Portland Thorns, a NWSL franchise in Oregon, has an average of seventeen thousand fans per game, more than three times the viewership average of other women's teams. Its fervent fan base was built from the loyal University of Portland spectators and organizational excellence.[135] The affiliation with a male counterpart team has also

---

132 "Can a Soccer Club Change the World?" Georgetown University School of Continuing Studies, August 2, 2017.

133 Elliot Turner, "Why MLS is completely justified in charging a $200 million expansion fee," SBNation, August 19, 2016.

134 Frank Pingue, "Women's soccer league gaining foothold in U.S.," Reuters, March 22, 2018.

135 Ibid.

helped. More than half of the NWLS franchises benefit from the existing organization, fan base, and stability.[136]

Most importantly, the female space is not a charity case. Female athletes and coaches continue to be paid less than their male counterparts. Some could argue that viewership, sport discipline, and fan base is a lot smaller than the male establishments, but men already have all the resources to their advantage. This inequality is driven by resourcing, not indicated by market signals as much of the world would like to believe.

When media started covering men very disproportionately, women started making a lot less than them.[137] In the '90s, media started pouring a lot more money into male sports coverage, contributing to driving a wedge in the gender pay gap.[138] As stated, "Women used to rank more prominently among the top-earning athletes, but over the past twenty-five years, media companies have spent billions on TV deals for live sports content. The result is an explosion in player salaries in the major men's sports leagues." So, it is likely the opposite, where media decided to put resources behind men instead of women, driving viewership away from female sports, rather than female sports being the cause of low viewership.

---

136 Ibid.

137 Charlotte Rogers, "Why brands must rethink their approach to women's sports sponsorship," MarketingWeek, February 8, 2018.

138 Olivia Abrams, "Why Female Athletes Earn Less Than Men Across Most Sports," Forbes, June 23, 2019.

Again, this is an active choice of resourcing much more than an unbreakable cycle of "there is no demand for female sports." Australia, for example, has found success in the Rebel Women's Big Bash League (WBBL), the Women's Australian Rules Football League (AFLW), and Suncorp Super Netball, which have all been drawing large audiences, revenues, and sponsorships. Early adopters to gender equity are expanding their investment or switching from men's to women's teams and later movers are coming in as club sponsorships. A report released by Nielsen Australia in 2019, states, "Women's sport has intangible association value. Around eight-in-ten (78%) female sports fans say it is important for sponsors to support women's sport; and 74% say companies involved in sponsoring sport gain in appeal with the audience."[139]

**BLACK ROSES**
It does take more than just brands or female athletes to continue to move the needle. It takes whole communities and teams.

I sought out Black Roses in the summer of 2019 and had a phenomenal experience joining a couple sessions. I was looking to instill some novel training into my routine and meet other athletes. Around that time, Black Roses held a series of "women's open sessions." These sessions specifically welcomed women only, which were then followed by general or co-ed open sessions. I was drawn to Black Roses not only because of the team's elusiveness, but also its pace. On paper,

---

[139] Monique Perry and Kayla Ramiscal, "Girl Power: Measuring the Rise of Women's Sports in Australia," Nielsen, June 3, 2019.

the crew seemed to only have a handful of athletes, who were all very fast. There was no golden ticket to join the "Roses"; it was through invite only, though they were very welcoming to anyone that wanted to drop into a session. Black Roses' social media presence was highly curated, with barely any leads on the full roster of the crew. I held them in high regard and wanted to train with them, even if it meant I was dead last.

By then, I was already a sponsored triathlete. Being a "sponsored athlete" was the culmination of working on this book as a way to process my interest in amateur sport sponsorship. It was not only a way to research and apply my learnings to myself, but also to understand the athlete and brand perspective in the sponsorship relationship. Running with Black Roses was a blip in my training, but also highly beneficial as a case study. I wouldn't call myself a running purist, so my participation was more so for exploratory purposes.

Black Roses is a running collective based on the idea that men and women could train side by side doing the same workout. True to the idea of the collective, Roses is very open to newcomers as long as you show up. The crew exudes a core identity as pure endurance runners. What I found is an unwavering faith that men and women could train side by side together, a strong sense of community contributing to the collective, and workouts that were nothing short of intense and required complete mental focus. The feel of the team is unilateral in strides and in style. The best in class street style crossed with blistering speedy track sessions.

Black Roses' philosophy for gender training parity isn't a difficult concept to grasp in the twenty-first century, especially in the liberal epicenter of NYC. Yet, when faced with the gender gap statistics, there is still a big perception gap, not to mention the pay gap as well.

Based on a market report from 2011 to 2013, female sport sponsorship expenditures made up a mere 0.4 percent of the total spending. According to Nielsen in the UK, between 2013 to 2017, the number of women's sport sponsored deals increased by 47 percent.[140] These statistics represent the highest level of athleticism for pros. It's hard to imagine that the trends aren't similar for amateur athletes who compete at levels lower than the best of the best for how far society is from equity. This may be a slight extrapolation, as there is limited information for amateur compensation as amateurs don't compete for money or play the sport professionally.

It takes broad cultural acceptance and work at every level, from amateur to professional, and the supporting environment to move toward equality.

## SUIT UP

The most covered fight for compensation equality has been equal pay for the US Women's National Team. Women have been vocal about equal pay, especially when they bring in the titles and championship wins. Two years after the fight for compensation equity, the US Women's Soccer Team signed a new collective bargaining agreement. The deal outlines increased salary and bonus compensation as well

---

140 Charlotte Rogers, "Why brands must rethink their approach to wom-en's sports sponsorship," MarketingWeek, February 8, 2018.

as travel, pregnancy, and adoption benefits that the men's national team receives.[141] The complaint filed by the Women's National team states:

> "Female WNT players would earn a maximum of $99,000 or $4,950 per game, while similarly situated male MNT players would earn an average of $263,320 or $13,166 per game."[142]

In August of 2019, after another World Cup Championship, few headwinds have been made. USWNT has pulled in $1.87 million more for US soccer than the USMNT since 2016. The men's team was paid $5.8 million in 2014 for making it as far as round 16 that year, whereas the women's team won the World Cup in Canada in 2015 and only made $1.7 million.[143] It wasn't until November 2019, when a court date was set for May 2020 and the case moved forward as a class action lawsuit, did the fight for equality move in the right direction.

---

141  Graham Hays, "U.S. Soccer, women's national team ratify new CBA," ESPN, April 5, 2017.

142  Morgan et al v. US Soccer Federation, Inc, Case No. 2:19-CV-01717 (2019)

143  Ryan Lake, "USWNT Fight for Equality in the U.S. While Taking on the World in the World Cup," Forbes, July 2, 2019.

The other women's professional teams are seeking advice and following suit.[144]

The WNBA did recently add a multiyear partnership with CBS Sports Network to air forty games next season, and the new pact is in addition to the league's existing deal with ESPN. More TV exposure for the players will lead to more visibility, and more visibility could lead to major deals with endorsers in the future. Nike hasn't made a signature shoe for a WNBA player in over twenty years.[145]

In January 2020, the WNBA agreed to double the salary ceiling and provide maternity leave.[146]

Women being granted the same sport representation as men was never a given. Unfortunately, the amount of exposure is highly correlated with how much money is at stake. Monetary spoils default to the men first. Look around to which gender gets the most sports coverage. How many "bests" in male world class athletes can you name versus the number of female world class athletes? The good thing is, the trend is shifting toward female sports coverage. As the number of women participating in sports increases and women are shifting toward controlling more of the purchasing power, brands are starting to take notice. Nike, Visa, and Secret

---

144 Andrew Das, "In Fight for Equality, U.S. Women's Soccer Team Leads the Way," NY Times, March 4, 2018.

145 Kellen Becoats, "WNBA Sneaker Culture Deserves More Respect," Sports Illustrated, August 28, 2018.

146 Howard Megdal, "W.N.B.A. Makes 'Big Bet on Women' With a New Contract," NY Times. January 14, 2020.

came out in support of the US Women's National Soccer Team's litigation for equal pay, understanding the current tide in consumer sentiment.[147]

Corporations can shift their investments to promote gender equality through sport sponsorship at every level, from grassroots to professional. The marrying of brands and elite amateur athletes can create markets where both athletes and companies benefit from the relationship. Ultimately, sponsorship could be the avenue to bridge the gender pay gap and elevate the voice and accomplishments of female athletes.

---

147 Kevin Draper, "Pushed by Consumers, Some Sponsors Join Soccer's Fight Over Equal Pay," NY Times, August 5, 2019.

## ELEVEN

A cyclical nature of sports exists. Eat, sleep, train; eat, sleep, train. Everything comes full circle.

Triathlon is an expensive sport. It is also a lonely sport. I train by myself for hours and get up early in the morning to hit the sessions. It is no different for many of my competitors.

When I started in 2018, I really went from zero to sixty. In that year, I did four Olympics, one half, and one full distance race. To jump from Olympic to full distance that fast is actually very unheard of. What pushed me to progress in this expedited fashion was rookie strategy. I figured that I was young and had certain things going my way: no obligations like young kids, a significant other, or ailing parents. Being in the 18–24 age group, I was also in a more lenient and not as cut-throat bracket.

What kept me in the sport was my love for discipline and seeing the opportunity for community involvement. I was intrigued by the sponsorship potential between amateur athletes and brands and figured I could apply it to my own career.

To start, I didn't have much of a digital presence. The "Great Millennial Migration" off Facebook had already happened, I wasn't an avid Instagram user, and could not comprehend

Twitter, TikTok, or the myriad of other platforms. Understanding I was a bit of a Luddite in the digital age, I needed at least some intentional improvements.

Being an Instagram influencer wasn't the goal and neither was doing things for the "'gram." To be frank, I don't think it ever should be. In the back of my mind, I carve out what I wanted to share with all these brands. It was small steps: engage with the community, post and tag brands, and accumulate race results. I figured I could do simple things to make a stronger case that I could bring value to a team during application season in the fall.

As I was figuring out the social media landscape within triathlon, that platform also became my guide—let the social media snooping and detective work ensue. I did my research and found one profile that lead to the next, and I observed. I saw how people commented, liked, and what their presence was like. How do ambassadors represent the brand? This drove insights to what the brand was looking for. At the end of the day, the athletes are a mouthpiece for the brand. This was before I knew brands also needed individual athletes to add personality to their brand content.

I then created a spreadsheet and tracked team application release dates and deadlines. To me, they were like college applications. I was pretty cognizant of not applying to teams where I knew I wouldn't take the sponsored spot. I could gauge whether I identified with the brand by looking at their brand ambassadors and digital footprint. Wattie Ink became the frontrunner, as I was already repping them. I raced in all of their gear, I tagged them, I liked and shared a lot of their posts, and engaged with their team members.

So, the story goes like this: Wattie Ink had two teams, and it released the Hitsquad team applications before the Elite applications in a similar format. It was a bit confusing, so I actually got on the Hitsquad team first, and then realized that I wanted to be on the Elite team. I rescinded my application for the Hitsquad and then reapplied for the Elite squad, using the exact same application. Luckily enough, Wattie Ink inducted me onto the Elite team.

The application decision announcement was made on a random day in November 2018, and I was actually in a late afternoon work meeting. I pulled up my emails during the meeting and saw in ginormous font, "TIME TO ROCK." I'm pretty sure I had the goofiest smile plastered on my face. Kind of embarrassing as my mind was racing, while I was taking part in this pretty large meeting. A complete hot flash came over me as I was so excited that I wanted to tell everyone in my vicinity that I got on the team. My coworkers were pretty understanding, but I'm not actually sure if they truly understood my sentiment or most likely just thought this girl went off the rails.

Almost immediately, I was inundated with virtual welcomes from the strong Wattie Ink community. The welcomes consisted of friend requests and tags to bring newbies into the fold. It was a pretty awesome digital experience, as teammates are spread all across the continental US and Canada.

Working on this book coincided with my sponsorship journey. This book has been a way to synthesize the lessons from both the brand and athlete side. But even more than that, it's meant to encourage the symbiotic relationships between brands and amateur athletes. Brands and athletes can bring a lot to the table. Brands now leverage brand ambassadors to build their presence and engage with potential customers. Athletes can lean on brands to further their athletic careers and get involved in the larger sport community.

That community-centric mindset was what I came onto the team with. I wanted to continue to invest in the community that welcomed me with open arms. Sponsorship isn't a freebie; it's lot more work than people expect it to be. A lot of people interested in sponsorship are usually decent athletes, even elite athletes. But sponsorship is a relationship that needs constant investment. It's not just about getting sponsored stuff. It can't just be taking and not giving. People who do it very well create a virtuous cycle for everyone to reap more benefits. At the end of the day, the brand-athlete relationship should be mutually beneficial, if not, a positive externality for the larger sports community. It's a full team effort to provide value for a brand and enable it to continue sponsoring amateur athletes.

Rock the W. I hope you can win at your sponsorship endeavors.

# APPENDIX

**CHAPTER 1**

"Chapter 5: Grit." Run Wild. Jay Bird, November 2018.

Elder, Adam. "The Rise of Run Crews." Motiv Sports, December 4, 2017. https://www.motivrunning.com/running-life/running-culture/rise-run-crews/.

Lappe, Meg. "Inside the Black Roses: NYC's Fastest and Most Elusive Run Club." Gear Patrol. Gear Patrol, May 10, 2018. https://gearpatrol.com/2018/05/10/black-roses-profile/.

**CHAPTER 2**

Locke, Susannah. "The Science of Choking under Pressure—and How to Avoid It." Vox. Vox, August 4, 2016. https://www.vox.com/2014/11/14/7209383/rio-olympics-2016-choke-pressure-psychology-sports.

Montero, Barbara Gail. "The Myth of 'Just Do It'." The New York Times. The New York Times, June 10, 2013. https://opinionator.blogs.nytimes.com/2013/06/09/the-myth-of-just-do-it/.

"With Brain Science, Doubt Can Be a Distant Memory." The Washington Post. WP Company, May 24, 2016. https://www.washingtonpost.com/sf/brand-connect/strayer/brain-science/.

編輯群. "鐵人之花—汪旖文的凱旋之路." Don1Don, May 7, 2018. http://www.don1don.com/archives/103839/鐵人之花汪旖文的凱旋之路

## CHAPTER 3

"150,000 Subscriber Update!" YouTube. YouTube, May 25, 2018. https://www.youtube.com/watch?v=pOrJWKz6i3A.

Blewitt, Mike. "Sonya Looney Leaves Topeak Ergon to Start Her Own Project." MarathonMTB.com, January 6, 2015. https://marathonmtb.com/2015/01/06/sonya-looney-leaves-topeak-ergon-to-start-her-own-project/.

"I Quit My Job Three Years Ago and You Kept This Channel Going." YouTube. YouTube, September 27, 2019. https://www.youtube.com/watch?v=5DSDOkeqm70.

Facebook. Wattie Ink, July 11, 2019. https://www.facebook.com/codybeals/videos/10162079234400445/?q=team wattie ink social channel cody beals&epa=SEARCH_BOX.

Kennedy, Brian. "The BKXC Origin Story." BKXC. BKXC, July 27, 2016. https://bkxc.bike/news/2017/5/15/the-bkxc-origin-story.

Kennedy, Brian. "The Three Laws of YouTube: How I Picked Up 1,000 Subscribers in 100 Days." BKXC. BKXC, July 27, 2016. https://bkxc.bike/news/2017/5/15/the-three-laws-of-youtube-or-how-i-got-to-1000-subscribers-in-100-days.

Looney, Sonya. "Meet Sonya." Sonya Looney. Accessed January 27, 2020. https://www.sonyalooney.com/sonyas-story/.

"Sonya Looney—24h World Champion." Stages Cycling—North America, October 6, 2016. *https://stagescycling.com/us/news/ sonya-looney-crowned-24-hour-world-champion/*.

"The Funding Problem in Sports." Peakz, December 20, 2019. *https://peakz.com/en/the-funding-problem/*.

"USA Triathlon Demographics." Team USA. Accessed November 10, 2019. *https://www.teamusa.org/usa-triathlon/about/ multisport/demographics*.

## CHAPTER 4

"2013-14 Women's XC/Track Roster." Georgetown University Athletics. Accessed November 15, 2019. *http://guhoyas.com/ sports/womens-track-and-field/roster/kirsten-kasper/7938*.

Baker, Joseph, Sean Horton, Jennifer Robertson-Wilson, and Michael Wall. "Nurturing Sport Expertise: Factors Influencing the Development of Elite Athlete." Journal of Sports Science & Medicine. March 1, 2003. *https://www.ncbi. nlm.nih.gov/pmc/articles/PMC3937568/*.

Bike. "Rebecca Rusch Partners with Niner Bikes." BIKE Magazine. BIKE Magazine, January 21, 2015. *https://www. bikemag.com/industry-news/rebecca-rusch-partners-niner- bikes/*.

Cushionbury, Mike. "Endurance Legend Rebecca Rusch Signs with Niner Bikes · Dirt Rag." Dirt Rag, January 21, 2015. *https://dirtragmag.com/articles/endurance-legend-rebecca- rusch-signs-with-niner-bikes/*.

Dure, Beau. "Summer Rappaport Clinches Olympic Triathlon Berth in Tumultuous Qualifier—OlympicTalk: NBC Sports." OlympicTalk | NBC Sports, August 15, 2019. *https://olympics. nbcsports.com/2019/08/14/summer-rappaport-clinches- olympic-triathlon-berth-in-qualifier-marred-by-heat-and-a- crash/*.

"Kirsten Kasper." Santara Group. Accessed November 15, 2019. *https://www.santaragroup.com/athletes/kirsten-kasper.*

"Letting Go, Slowing Down and Trusting Others: Rebecca Rusch Reflects on the Making of Blood Road." Niner Bikes, July 18, 2017. *https://ninerbikes.com/blogs/niner-blog/rebecca-rusch-reflects-on-blood-road.*

"Liv and Giant USA Announce Partnership with Rebecca Rusch." YouTube. YouTube, January 22, 2020. *https://www.youtube.com/watch?v=99g8yA9jyrI.*

"Summer Rappaport Qualifies For 2020 Tokyo Olympic Games." Triathlete, August 15, 2019. *https://www.triathlete.com/2019/08/news/summer-rappaport-qualifies-for-2020-tokyo-olympic-games_382159.*

**CHAPTER 5**

Felton, Ryan. "Faraday Future Is Even Getting Sued by a Bicycle Company." Jalopnik. Jalopnik, April 26, 2017. *https://jalopnik.com/faraday-future-is-even-getting-sued-by-a-bicycle-compan-1794680086.*

Frothingham, Steve. "Trek Sued over Use of the Farley Name on Fat Bikes." Bicycle Retailer and Industry News, September 15, 2017. *https://www.bicycleretailer.com/north-america/2017/09/15/trek-sued-over-use-farley-name-fat-bikes#.Xi7jKZPonBJ.*

"Lauren Gregg's Custom Ford Transit Van." Pinkbike, May 19, 2016. *https://www.pinkbike.com/news/lauren-greggs-custom-ford-transit-van-2016.html.*

"Now You Know." Drunkcyclist.com, March 12, 2014. *http://drunkcyclist.com/2014/03/12/now-know/.*

"Solo Becomes 5010." Santa Cruz Bicycles. Santa Cruz Bicycles, September 24, 2014. https://www.santacruzbicycles.com/en-US/news/422.

"Super Hybrid Cars." TrendHunter.com. TREND HUNTER Inc., June 26, 2008. https://www.trendhunter.com/trends/antro-solo.

## CHAPTER 6

Almquist, Eric, and Tamar Dane Dor-Ner. "Brand Strategy That Shifts Demand: Less Buzz, More Economics." Bain, November 14, 2014. https://www.bain.com/insights/brand-strategy-that-shifts-demand/.

"Ambassadors." Lululemon. Accessed December 20, 2019. https://shop.lululemon.com/ambassadors/_/N-1z141e2.

"American Bicycle Group Moves to Larger Facility." Bicycle Retailer and Industry News, August 9, 2016. https://www.bicycleretailer.com/north-america/2016/08/09/american-bicycle-group-moves-larger-facility#.XXv6apNKiYU.

Fernandez, Chantal. "Inside Lululemon's Unconventional Influencer Network." Fashionista, November 2, 2016. https://fashionista.com/2016/11/lululemon-ambassadors.

Finanger, Lars. "Kona Dreamin' with Zwift's Academy Tri Team." slowtwich.com, October 12, 2019. https://www.slowtwitch.com/Interview/Kona_Dreamin_with_Zwift_s_Academy_Tri_Team_7455.html.

Finanger, Lars. "The High Flying Women of Zwift's Academy Triathlon Team." slowtwich.com, October 24, 2019. https://www.slowtwitch.com/Interview/The_High_Flying_Women_of_Zwift_s_Academy_Triathlon_Team_7472.html.

Gary. "Specialized Zwift Academy Tri Returns for 2019." endurancebusiness.com, December 21, 2018. https://www.

endurancebusiness.com/2018/industry-news/specialized-zwift-academy-tri-returns-for-2019/.

"Got What it Takes to Get on the Brand New Zwift Specialized Tri Team?" Triathlete, February 23, 2018. https://www.triathlete.com/2018/02/news/got-takes-get-brand-new-zwift-specialized-tri-team_310986.

Harby, Chris. "Bex Rimmington Interview: Unfinished Business for Melton's Iron Lady." Melton Times, December 27, 2018. https://www.meltontimes.co.uk/sport/more-sport/bex-rimmington-interview-unfinished-business-for-melton-s-iron-lady-1-8748048.

Hehemann, Nick. "Age Group Triathlete of the Year Justin Lippert Is Going 'Full Send' into 2019." Team USA, May 3, 2019. https://www.teamusa.org/USA-Triathlon/News/Articles-and-Releases/2019/May/03/Age group-Triathlete-of-the-Year-Justin-Lippert-is-Going-Full-Send-into-2019.

"Introducing the 2018 Specialized Zwift Academy Tri Team!" YouTube. YouTube, April 24, 2018. https://www.youtube.com/watch?v=kfUCRXJxoSo.

"IRONMAN TriClub Program—Americas." Wattie Ink. had the most members racing...—IRONMAN TriClub Program—Americas, October 29, 2019. https://www.facebook.com/TriClubAmericas/photos/a.1761720980726394/2534543410110810/?type=3&theater.

Krabel, Herbert. "On the throttle with Kona superstar Ruth Purbrook." slowtwich.com, October 21, 2019. https://www.slowtwitch.com/Interview/On_the_throttle_with_Kona_superstar_Ruth_Purbrook_7470.html.

Lutz, Ashley. "Lululemon Calls Its Ideal Customers 'Ocean' and 'Duke'—Here's Everything We Know About Them." Business Insider. Business Insider, February 2, 2015. https://www.

businessinsider.com/lululemon-idea-customers-ocean-and-duke-2015-2.

Norfleet, Rachael. Instagram post. October 14, 2018. https://www.instagram.com/p/Bo7Vl2zhFeG/.

Overholt, Zach. "Factory Tour: Litespeed Celebrates 30 Years of Cutting Edge Titanium Bicycle Manufacturing." Bikerumor, February 19, 2016. https://bikerumor.com/2016/02/19/factory-tour-litespeed-celebrates-30-years-of-cutting-edge-titanium-bicycle-manufacturing/.

"Quintana Roo and Wattie Ink Enter into Tri Team Partnership." Endurancebusiness.com, June 4, 2019. https://www.endurancebusiness.com/2019/industry-news/quintana-roo-and-wattie-ink-enter-into-tri-team-partnership/.

Schlange, Eric. "XP, Levels, and Unlocks in Zwift Ride." Zwift Insider, October 23, 2019. https://zwiftinsider.com/points-levels-unlocks/.

"The 2019 Specialized Zwift Academy Tri Team Training Camp" YouTube. YouTube, May 25, 2019. https://www.youtube.com/watch?v=siJhtaweo-c.

"We Were Totally Wrong About Zwift Academy." Triathlete, December 22, 2018. https://www.triathlete.com/2018/12/news/we-were-totally-wrong-about-zwift-academy_338272.

## CHAPTER 7

"American Bicycle Group Moves to Larger Facility." Bicycle Retailer and Industry News, August 9, 2016. https://www.bicycleretailer.com/north-america/2016/08/09/american-bicycle-group-moves-larger-facility#.XXv6apNKiYU.

Beals, Cody. "Ventum & My Quest for a Worthy Whip." Cody Beals, January 18, 2016. http://www.codybeals.com/2016/01/ventum-my-quest-for-a-worthy-whip/.

Clutton, Graham. "London 2012 Olympics: Modern Pentathlon Star Heather Fell Cannot Face Prospect of Missing Out on Final Shot at Gold." The Telegraph. Telegraph Media Group, April 5, 2012. https://www.telegraph.co.uk/sport/olympics/modern-pentathlon/9186861/London-2012-Olympics-modern-pentathlon-star-Heather-Fell-cannot-face-prospect-of-missing-out-on-final-shot-at-gold.html.

Facebook. Wattie Ink, July 11, 2019. https://www.facebook.com/codybeals/videos/10162079234400445/?q=team wattie ink social channel cody beals&epa=SEARCH_BOX.

"Heather Fell." Global Triathlon Network. Accessed January 28, 2020. https://www.globaltrinetwork.com/presenters/heather-fell.

"Heather Fell." Team GB. Accessed January 27, 2020. https://www.teamgb.com/athletes/heather-fell.

"Heather Fell Announces Retirement from Modern Pentathlon." BBC Sport. BBC, January 9, 2014. https://www.bbc.com/sport/modern-pentathlon/25668102.

Ingle, Sean. "London 2012: Heather Fell Fears Abrupt End to Her High-Five Dream." The Guardian. Guardian News and Media, March 24, 2012. https://www.theguardian.com/sport/2012/mar/24/london-2012-heather-fell-modern-pentathlon.

Overholt, Zach. "Factory Tour: Litespeed Celebrates 30 Years of Cutting Edge Titanium Bicycle Manufacturing." Bikerumor, February 19, 2016. https://bikerumor.com/2016/02/19/factory-tour-litespeed-celebrates-30-years-of-cutting-edge-titanium-bicycle-manufacturing/.

"Quintana Roo and Wattie Ink Enter into Tri Team Partnership." Endurancebusiness.com, June 4, 2019. https://www.endurancebusiness.com/2019/industry-news/quintana-roo-and-wattie-ink-enter-into-tri-team-partnership/.

Rotella, Mark, Sarah F Gold, Lynn Andriani, Michael Scharf, and Emily Chenoweth. "THE PARTNERSHIP CHARTER: How to Start Out Right with Your New Business Partnership (or Fix the One You're In)." Publisher Weekly, June 28, 2004.

Sauer, Paul J. "How to Work with a Partner (Year After Year After Year)." Inc. Magazine, Oct 2004.

@wattieink. Instagram post. May 7, 2019. https://www.instagram.com/p/BxKz8NAHGfT/?utm_source=ig_web_copy_link.

**CHAPTER 8**

Bagg, Chris. "Wattie Ink. Turns Ten" Wattie Ink (blog), December 11, 2019. https://www.wattieink.com/blogs/blog/wattie-ink-and-the-elite-team-turn-ten.

Bagg, Chris. "Join the W Family – Applications Open Today." Wattie Ink (blog), Sept 24, 2019. https://www.wattieink.com/blogs/blog/join-the-wattie-ink-teams-applications-open-today.

Coombs, Danielle Sarver, and Bob Batchelor. American History through American Sports: From Colonial Lacrosse to Extreme Sports. Vol. 1. ABC-CLIO, 2012.

"CALLING TOP LEVEL ATHLETES: SUUNTO'S NEW MULTISPORT TEAM IS RECRUITING!", Suunto, November 27, 2018.

Francis, Trista. Instagram post. Dec 28, 2018. https://www.instagram.com/p/Br8jQFrBJFV/?utm_source=ig_web_copy_link.

"It's Who We Are—The Wattie Ink. Story." Wattie Ink. Accessed January 27, 2020. https://www.wattieink.com/pages/about-us.

Patterson, Troy. "Why Timex Is the Best Watch for the Money." Bloomberg, March 9, 2019. https://www.bloomberg.com/news/articles/2017-03-09/why-timex-is-the-best-watch-for-the-money.

Timex. Accessed July 15, 2019. http://www.timexteam.com/.

"Timex, Walt Disney, Mickey Mantle & the Ironman Triathlon Watch." Ironman Triathlon Watch—A History of the Timex Company. Accessed January 27, 2020. https://ironmantriathlonwatchsite.weebly.com/index.html.

"THE ORIGINS OF THE TIMEX IRONMAN WATCH." cbw.com, August 28, 2019. https://www.cbw.com/articles_csezda.html.

### CHAPTER 9

"48 Hours of Training with Tim Don" YouTube. YouTube, May 31, 2011. https://www.youtube.com/watch?v=0BaDYnpTA2Y.

"Athletes." Red Bull. Accessed January 27, 2020. https://www.redbull.com/us-en/athletes.

Chase, Lisa. "Free Solo's Director Doesn't Give a F**k About Climbing." Outside Online, September 12, 2018. https://www.outsideonline.com/2342126/Elizabeth-Chai-Vasarhelyi-free-solo-movie.

"Company." Red Bull. Accessed January 27, 2020. http://energydrink-us.redbull.com/en/company.

Dumont, Guillaume. "The Beautiful and the Damned." Journal of Sport and Social Issues 41, no. 2 (April 2017): 99–117.

"Felix Baumgartner's supersonic freefall from 128k'—Mission Highlights." YouTube. YouTube, Oct 14, 2012. https://www.youtube.com/watch?v=FHtvDA0W34I.

"Getting 'It': What Brands Can Learn from Red Bull About Marketing in ESports." Digital Surgeons, April 17, 2018. https://www.digitalsurgeons.com/thoughts/strategy/getting-it-what-brands-can-learn-from-red-bull-about-marketing-in-esports/.

Gschwandtner, Gerhard. "The Powerful Sales Strategy Behind Red Bull." Selling Power, March 1, 2012. https://www.sellingpower.com/2012/03/01/9437/the-powerful-sales-strategy-behind-red-bull.

Guerrasio, Jason. "The Directors of Oscar-Winning Documentary 'Free Solo' Explain Why They Made the Risky Decision to Film Alex Honnold's 3,000 Foot Climb up El Capitan without a Rope." Business Insider, February 24, 2019. https://www.businessinsider.com/free-solo-documentary-directors-interview-filming-alex-honnold-el-capitan-climb-without-rope-2018-9.

Honnold Foundation. Accessed January 27, 2020. http://www.honnoldfoundation.org/about.

"I QUIT MY JOB! || Vlog 1" YouTube. YouTube, August 31, 2017. https://www.youtube.com/watch?v=mzCCoEGxyaA.

Jutkowitz, Alexander. "The Content Marketing Revolution." Harvard Business Review, July 1, 2013. https://hbr.org/2014/07/the-content-marketing-revolution.

O'Brien, James. "How Red Bull Takes Content Marketing to the Extreme." Mashable, December 19, 2012. https://mashable.com/2012/12/19/red-bull-content-marketing/.

O'Connor, Ashling. "Felix Baumgartner's plunge from stratosphere breaks broadcast records." The Australian, October 16, 2012. https://www.theaustralian.com.au/news/world/felix-baumgartners-plunge-from-stratosphere-breaks-broadcast-records/news-story/204e359cb84e66cc215b9fce5b28f074.

"Olé | The Ryan Hall Boston Marathon Workout" YouTube. YouTube, April 22, 2009. https://www.youtube.com/watch?v=QbKp2HeUpkY.

"Red Bull Invests $65M on Space Jump as More Than 8 Million Watch on YouTube." Sport Business Daily. October 16, 2012. *https://www.sportsbusinessdaily.com/Global/Issues/2012/10/16/Marketing-and-Sponsorship/Red-Bull.aspx.*

"Red Bull Stratos." Red Bull Stratos (blog). Accessed January 27, 2020. *http://www.redbullstratos.com/blog/post/101027346292.html.*

"Red Bull Stratos – World Record Freefall." YouTube. YouTube, October 15, 2012. *https://www.youtube.com/watch?v=dOoHArAzdug&list=PLnuf8iyXggLFKnC1bJVA1YO8e-eP-ntHd.*

"Talbot Cox." Marni on the Move (podcast), August 11, 2018. *https://marnionthemove.com/tag/talbot-cox/.*

"Talbot Cox" YouTube, accessed January 27, 2020. *https://www.youtube.com/user/talbotcox44/videos.*

"What Is Content Marketing?" Content Marketing Institution. Accessed January 27, 2020. *https://contentmarketinginstitute.com/what-is-content-marketing/.*

Wieners, Brad. "Q: When Is a Cliff Dive Good for Sales? A: When it's Sponsored by Red Bull." Bloomberg, May 25, 2013. *https://www.bloomberg.com/news/articles/2013-05-25/q-when-is-a-cliff-dive-good-for-sales-a-when-its-sponsored-by-red-bull.*

Zmuda, Natalie. "Red Bull's Stratos 'Space Jump' Wowed the World—While Selling a Lot of Products." Ad Age, September 2, 2013. *https://adage.com/article/special-report-marketer-alist-2013/red-bull-stratos-space-jump-helped-sell-a-lot-product/243751.*

**CHAPTER 10**

Abrams, Olivia. "Why Female Athletes Earn Less Than Men Across Most Sports." Forbes. June 23, 2019. *https://www.*

*forbes.com/sites/oliviaabrams/2019/06/23/why-female-athletes-earn-less-than-men-across-most-sports/#423a5dc40fbe.*

"Adrienne Lofton, Under Armour." Sports Business Journal. September 11, 2017. *https://www.sportsbusinessdaily.com/ Journal/Issues/2017/09/11/Game-Changers/Adrienne-Lofton. aspx.*

Axon, Rachel. "Sarah Burke left lasting legacy on Olympics before death." USA Today, February 18, 2014. *https://www. usatoday.com/story/sports/olympics/sochi/2014/02/18/sarah-burke-lasting-legacy-womens-skiing-halfpipe-debut/5585085/.*

Becoats, Kellen. "WNBA Sneaker Culture Deserves More Respect." Sports Illustrated. August 28, 2018. *https://www. si.com/wnba/2018/08/28/wnba-sneaker-culture-maya-moore-tamara-young-breanna-stewart-nike-jordan-adidas-puma.*

"Can a Soccer Club Change the World?" Georgetown University School of Continuing Studies, August 2, 2017. *https://scs. georgetown.edu/news-and-events/article/6534/can-soccer-club-change-world-georgetown-and-fc-barcelona-will-give-it-try.*

Das, Andrew. "In Fight for Equality, U.S. Women's Soccer Team Leads the Way." NY Times. March 4, 2018. *https://www. nytimes.com/2018/03/04/sports/soccer/us-womens-soccer-equality.html.*

Donaldson, Amy. "Sarah Burke Succumbs to Ski Injuries." Deseret News, January 19, 2012. *https://www.deseret. com/2012/1/19/20245925/sarah-burke-succumbs-to-ski-injuries#this-jan-16-2010-photo-shows-sarah-burke-reacting-after-a-run-during-the-womens-ski-halfpipe-finals-in-hunts-ville-utah-burke-succumbed-to-injuries-thursday-that-she-sustained-in-a-fall-while-training-in-the-superpipe-at-park-city-mountain-resort.*

Draper, Kevin. "Pushed by Consumers, Some Sponsors Join Soccer's Fight Over Equal Pay." NY Times. August 5, 2019. https://www.nytimes.com/2019/08/05/sports/soccer/womens-soccer-nike-sponsors.html.

Hays, Graham. "U.S. Soccer, women's national team ratify new CBA." ESPN. April 5, 2017. https://www.espn.com/espnw/sports/story/_/id/19082314/us-soccer-women-national-team-ratify-new-cba.

Lake, Ryan. "USWNT Fight for Equality in the U.S. While Taking on the World in the World Cup." Forbes. July 2, 2019. https://www.forbes.com/sites/ryanlake/2019/07/02/uswnt-fight-for-equality-in-the-us-while-taking-on-the-world-in-the-world-cup/#4090c3267b68.

Megdal, Howard. "W.N.B.A. Makes 'Big Bet on Women' With a New Contract." NY Times. January 14, 2020. https://www.nytimes.com/2020/01/14/sports/basketball/wnba-contract-collective-bargaining-agreement.html.

Morgan et al v. US Soccer Federation, Inc, Case No. 2:19-CV-01717 (2019), https://int.nyt.com/data/documenthelper/653-us-womens-soccer-complaint/f9367608e2eaf10873f4/optimized/full.pdf#page=1.

Perry, Monique and Kayla Ramiscal. "Girl Power: Measuring the Rise of Women's Sports in Australia." Nielsen. June 3, 2019.https://www.nielsen.com/au/en/insights/article/2019/girl-power-measuring-the-rise-of-women-s-sport-in-australia/.

Pingue, Frank. "Women's soccer league gaining foothold in U.S." Reuters. March 22, 2018. https://www.reuters.com/article/us-soccer-women-usa/womens-soccer-league-gaining-foothold-in-u-s-idUSKBN1GY2OE.

Rogers, Charlotte. "Why brands must rethink their approach to women's sports sponsorship." MarketingWeek. February

8, 2018. *https://www.marketingweek.com/brands-neglecting-womens-sports-sponsorship/*.

"Sponsorship Spending Trends, 2014-2018 (Predicted)." Marketing Charts. Accessed January 27, 2020. *https://www.marketingcharts.com/cross-media-and-traditional/sponsorships-traditional-and-cross-channel-82185/attachment/esp-global-sponsorship-spending-trends-2014-2018-feb2018*.

"Sponsorship Spending Report." IEG. 2015. *https://www.sponsorship.com/IEG/files/4e/4e525456-b2b1-4049-bd51-03d9c35ac507.pdf*.

Turner, Elliot. "Why MLS is completely justified in charging a $200 million expansion fee." SBNation. August 19, 2016. *https://www.sbnation.com/soccer/2016/8/9/12404638/mls-expansion-fee-number-of-teams-200-million*.

www.ingramcontent.com/pod-product-compliance
Lightning Source LLC
LaVergne TN
LVHW011835060526
838200LV00053B/4038